Religion Education And Life

Junior assembly book

Sandra Palmer and Elizabeth Breuilly

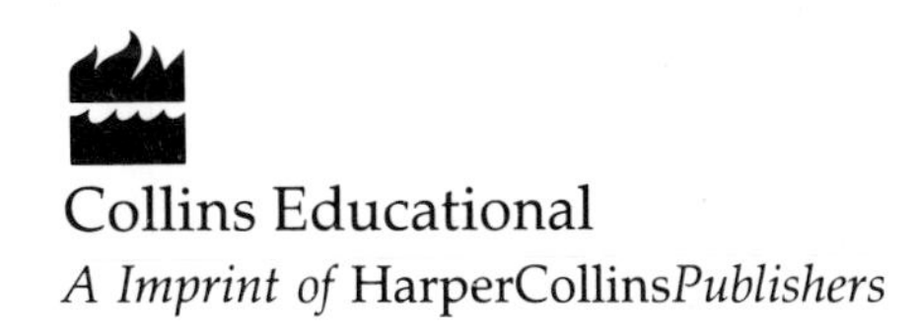

Published 1993 by CollinsEducational
an imprint of HarperCollins*Publishers*
77-85 Fulham Palace Road
Hammersmith
London W6 8JB

Reprinted 1994, 1996, 1998

ISBN 0 00 312002 3

© ICOREC
The authors assert the moral right to be identified as the authors of this work.

All rights reserved. No part of this publication may be reproduced, stored in a retrieval system, or transmitted, in any form or by any means, electronic, mechanical, photocopying, recording or otherwise, without the permission of Collins Educational.

Design by Derek Lee
Cover design by Leigh Hurlock
Cover artwork by Alice Bradbury

Typeset in Great Britain by Wyvern Typesetting Ltd, Bristol.
Printed and bound by Martins the Printers Berwick upon Tweed.

CONTENTS

INTRODUCTION

In this introduction are questions we feel may be in teachers' minds when using this material; the answers here should help to explain our approach to religious education. Though this book is full of stimulating ideas for assemblies, these are not randomly collected but have a coherent and consistent basis underpinning them.

This assembly book accompanies the *REAL Junior Teacher's Handbook* and develops work from the *REAL Infant Teacher's Handbook* and *REAL Infant Assembly Book*.

What is the understanding of worship in the book?

Our understanding of school worship is that it should be a time for the school to come together as a community, to celebrate as a community and to grow as a community. Thus, in this book, we have included ideas for the commemoration of events and for the celebration of shared values. Growth is not always comfortable, so the book contains assemblies which challenge preconceptions, when children may be taken by surprise, and will go away thinking and puzzling about what they have heard. They will also, we hope, go away sometimes moved, sometimes sorrowing, because some of these assemblies reflect the pain that is part of the fabric of our world and of children's lives.

This understanding of worship in school is a reflection of many aspects of worship in a Christian church. It is important to acknowledge this, because the law requires that school worship should be 'wholly or broadly Christian in character', without being distinctive of a particular Christian denomination. Christian worship, like the assemblies in this book, encompasses commemoration of events, celebration of events and a challenging and questioning element.

The main distinction between those participating in school worship and those participating in Christian worship, is that the latter is a corporate body of believers with a religious faith in common, the former is not. The law recognizes this in describing school worship as a collective rather than a corporate act. Therefore we have tried to use language which does not exclude non-Christians from full participation.

Is all the material in it Christian?

Yes and No. On the one hand, the assemblies themselves are all coherent with the Christian faith, expressing values and articulating questions which are central to it. On the other hand we have used material from a wide variety of sources – from folk tradition and non-Christian faiths – as Christian teachers and preachers have done for generations. (Jesus himself used stories from the Jewish folk tradition.) The guidelines to the 1988 Education Act recognize the possibility of using non-Christian material within the context of worship which is Christian in character.

What is the relationship between this book and the rest of REAL?

The Junior Teacher's Handbook

A major part of religious education is the study of religion, with the corresponding objective that children will grow in their understanding of it. The handbook offers ways of enabling children to do this. School worship may bring with it some understanding of religious belief and practice but this is incidental and not its primary purpose. It is therefore a mistake to think that religious education can take place satisfactorily through assemblies alone. This assembly book suggests ways of putting into the context of worship some of the themes of the handbook and some of the results of classroom studies. However, it also offers ideas for worship beyond those boundaries. Neither book, of course, attempts to offer a definitive content for RE.

There is a cross-reference table on p. 60 which shows clearly where the assemblies link with the Junior Handbook topics.

A Tapestry of Tales
This resource contains a wealth of stories from religious traditions, many of which will, we hope, challenge children's thinking in a manner not dissimilar to some of the story assemblies in this Junior Assembly Book. You may wish to use them in assembly in the same way that we have used the stories here.

The Infant Assembly Book
A number of themes in the Infant Assembly Book have been picked up in this Junior one, allowing both for development, and for the possibility of bringing infant and junior children together to celebrate a common theme, following separate input at their own level.

How do I use this book?

Some of the assemblies in this book require little preparation or resources, and can be lifted off the shelf. Others need time in the classroom beforehand as they involve children's work. All of them require you to think about creating the atmosphere in which they will take place. Christian worship is often an aesthetic experience, and we feel school worship should reflect this. Music, the use of tablecloths and wall hangings, artefacts, and pictures all contribute. Sometimes the mood created will be deliberately boisterous and joyful, at other times quiet and sombre, this will be dictated by the content of the assembly. The leader of the assembly also has a role to play in maintaining an atmosphere rather than deflating it by giving an extended commentary.

The recommended songs come from *The Complete Come and Praise*, compiled by Geoffrey Marshall Taylor (BBC Books, 1990) and *Alleluya! 77 Songs for Thinking People*, chosen by David Gadsby and John Hoggarth (A&C Black, 1980).

A word of caution, also. Whenever stories are used in a religious context it is often tempting to try and unpack a meaning for the children. Of course, we have a reason in mind for considering these stories worth telling, and we often explain this in the notes. You may see a particular worth and meaning yourself. But let the children make their own responses to the story instead of being told how to interpret it. For further discussion on story see *A Tapestry of Tales*.

Conclusion

The stories and 'assembly scripts' which we give in this book are not intended to be definitive texts which you must follow exactly as written. They are an offering to help you create your own way of communicating with the children.

We hope that this book will help you create assemblies which are qualitatively different from the rest of the school day, which draw the children and staff in to a common experience and a sharing of responses which will help build your school into a living and dynamic community where each has their part to play.

TIMES AND SEASONS

Assemblies to use at particular times of the year or festivals.

This section takes a variety of occasions, both secular and religious, and shows how their themes can be developed in assembly. They are intended as models which may give ideas about how other special occasions could be marked.

New School Year

The new school year is the time when the children are most aware of making a new start and preparing for the year ahead, and it is important to mark this in a way that is not too moralistic. We have taken up this theme by drawing on New Year ceremonies from different faiths. The Jewish New Year, Rosh Hashanah, falls at about this time, so we have used more material from this festival than from other new year celebrations. As part of the festival, the *shofar* (a ram's horn) is blown as a reminder to Jews to 'wake up', prepare for the new year, and reflect on their life. The theme of 'beginnings' is also taken up in the creation story from the Bible.

Purpose
to reflect on new beginnings, both at school and in a wider context.

Preparation
Find out the exact date of Rosh Hashanah if possible, as it varies slightly from year to year.

Prepare an 'alerting sound' (see below) – a car horn, bugle or shofar, for example.

In the class prepare a percussion accompaniment to the Genesis reading (see below).

Prepare also pictures or symbols for each of the days of creation.

Assembly
You could take up the theme of the shofar by using some loud 'alerting' noise, such as reveille played on a bugle, a car horn, or even a real shofar if you know someone who can blow it.

Then wish the children 'A Happy New Year!'

Leader:

> Although this is not the usual time for wishing a Happy New Year, it is the start of the year for the school, and it is good to celebrate that. There are many different New Year celebrations. Each of us start a 'new year' on our birthday. The Chinese start their New Year in February or March, and Jews start their New Year around now. At their New Year, Jews listen to the sound of a horn being blown, as a reminder to them to wake up, prepare for the year ahead, and think what their life is like. That's why we heard the [car horn, or whatever you used] just now – it's a signal to wake up and get ready.
>
> As well as thinking about their own lives at New Year, Jews also celebrate this time as the birthday of the world. When God created the world it was the very first New Year. Listen to the story of the birthday of the world.

Read the story of creation from Genesis 1–2:4. This could be greatly enhanced by the use of percussion instruments to illustrate and punctuate each 'day' of creation. The amount of preparation time available will dictate how much can be done here. Children could make pictures or symbols for each day.

> God created the world and saw that it was good, and so on the birthday of the world people give thanks to God for the good things in the world.

Sing 'Morning has Broken' (*Come and Praise* 1).

> In this New Year for our school, we too give thanks for the good things in the school, and

especially for the people who make the school – we give thanks for each other. For we are the school, not the buildings or the desks or the blackboards, and we have some new members of the school to greet and give thanks for.

Ask the new class entering the school to stand up, and give them a cheer.

Introduce any new members of staff, with perhaps a short interview about their interests, where they have come from, etc. Give them a cheer too.

And while you're about it, give a cheer for your school!

Prayer/reflection

Let us give thanks to God for the goodness of the world, and for our school. After every line, please say 'We thank you Lord'. (Or, if you feel this would conflict with the religious beliefs of some of the school, just 'We give thanks'.)

'For the earth and all things in it that are good,
We thank you Lord.
For this our school, for all who teach and work and learn within it,
We thank you Lord.
For the creation of men and women, girls and boys to be our friends and companions,
We thank you Lord.
For the new friends we will make this year,
We thank you Lord.
For this new year, for the new things we shall do and the new things we shall learn,
We thank you Lord.'

Songs

Come and Praise

11 For the beauty of the earth
9 Fill your hearts with joy and gladness
43 Give me oil in my lamp
47 One more step along the world I go

Preparation for Good Friday 1. God's Suffering

Primary children cannot be protected from the fact of suffering. All too often they meet it in their own experience; they see it on television and they will encounter it in the history programmes of study in the National Curriculum. They will also often see crucifixes, whether worn as pendants or as part of church architecture. These meditations acknowledge the presence of suffering, using the key Christian image of the crucifix as the focus.

The story of the crucifixion is central to Christianity, and in the *REAL Junior Teacher's Handbook* we concentrate on telling the story. Here we allow space to reflect on its meaning. The first Christians struggled to make sense of it, they believed that Jesus was the Messiah, the long-awaited one whom God had promised would be their deliverer. Why then did he die the death of an outcast, crucified as a criminal? They looked to the Hebrew prophets to find predictions that the Messiah would suffer (Isaiah 53) but these did not explain why the suffering of God's chosen one was necessary. One school of thought was that Jesus was punished instead of human beings. This is expressed clearly in words from Mrs Alexander's hymn 'There is a green hill far away' *Hymns Ancient and Modern New Standard* (Hymns Ancient and Modern, 1983):

> 'There was no other good enough to pay the
> price of sin;
> He only could unlock the gate
> Of heaven and let us in.'

Although this understanding of the crucifixion is popular in Western Christianity, this picture of a God demanding that someone must be punished to make forgiveness possible is one which is abhorred by many Christians who turn instead to other and often older ways of thinking about the significance of the cross. Christ's death, like much suffering in the world, is understood as a consequence of humanity's evil. It is seen as a place of reconciliation. God in Christ reaches out to humanity, to the world, to share its suffering and so be reconciled to it. He is the father who goes out to meet the prodigal son and share his burden.

There are of course, no neat explanations or formulas for understanding the mystery of the crucifixion. Thus the meaning is often explored in metaphor or folk tale. The following two assemblies are examples of this. Both are connected with nature, taking on the belief that Jesus died for the whole world (see John 3:16) and not just for humanity. They depend on children being familiar with the story of the crucifixion and resurrection so that they are in the context of hope. The stories are both beyond understanding in any full sense. They offer children an image or a way of seeing, to respond to in their own way. Given the sensitive nature of the first story it may be better for the cosier atmosphere of a class assembly rather than a full school assembly.

This assembly is adapted from a passage in Helen Waddell's book *Peter Abelard* (Constable and Co., 1933).

Purpose

to offer children one way of thinking about the death of Jesus, or one Christian response to the reality of suffering

Preparation

Collect two or more artists' pictures of the crucifixion.

Find a picture or a drawing of a tree trunk cut across the middle showing the rings.

Assembly

Remind children that Good Friday is approaching and that on that day Christians remember the death of Jesus on a cross. Explain to them that since that time Christians have tried to understand that death. The story is about two men trying to come to some understanding of it.

> Two men sat talking quietly in a hut by a river. One was called Abelard, one Thibault. They talked of the joys they had shared in the time they had known one another, and they spoke of the sorrow they had known.

Suddenly the evening air was pierced by a loud screech. They looked at each other and wondered what it was – a child perhaps. No, it couldn't be, not in this desolate place.

Together they rushed out of the hut, following the sound. There on the bank of the river they saw what had made the dreadful sound – a rabbit caught in a trap.

Abelard bent down and picked up the little creature, stroking its soft fur, comforting it as it breathed its last and died in his arms.

Tears filled his eyes. 'I saw it playing this afternoon,' he muttered, angrily. 'What did it ever do wrong? Why did it ever have to suffer like this? How can God be good and allow this?'

'I don't know,' replied Thibault. 'I don't know. I only believe that God is in this suffering. God shares and feels this suffering too.'

'You mean like when Jesus was on the cross. We saw God suffering on the cross,' said Abelard, looking up now at Thibault's worn face.

'That was only a glimpse of it,' continued Thibault. 'It was like when you cut across a tree. You see the rings at one place but they go right down into the tree. We saw God suffering in Jesus when he was crucified but he feels the pain of all his creation whenever it suffers.'

Abelard was silent, thinking of these words. Then the two men buried the rabbit beneath the autumn leaves and walked quietly back to the hut.

Prayer/reflection

Silence

Songs

Come and Praise

74 Sad, puzzled eyes
77 The sun burns hot and dry
85 Spirit of peace come to our waiting world
90 I come like a beggar with a gift in his hand

Follow-up

Talk with the children about their own feelings about suffering, and their own ideas of why people and creation suffer. This is best done in small groups, if possible.

Preparation for Good Friday 2. Saint Hubert

This story shows Christ suffering with creation but also reveals the cross as being a place of redemption. The story 'The Monkey Bridge' in *A Tapestry of Tales* has a similar theme and could be the basis of an assembly. This assembly would link with topic work on change.

See also the assembly on 'Icons' for a similar theme.

Purpose

to offer children a story which explores the significance of the crucifixion in terms of both the natural world, and the effect on the life of one man

Preparation

Find a picture of a stag.

There is an etching by Dürer of this story in the British Museum.

Assembly

Leader:

Hubert's delight in life was hunting. He loved the thrill of the hunt; galloping at top speed over fields, leaping over hedgerows and thundering off through the woods. He enjoyed the conquest of nature, the thrill when he rode home victorious with his day's killing.

One Good Friday he set forth for a good day's hunting. His servants were appalled. 'This of all days!' they said. 'This of all days you would go hunting! You should be praying and meditating on our Lord's crucifixion.'

But Hubert was not to be dissuaded. It was a bright, crisp, spring morning, just ideal for hunting.

He soon spotted a stag, magnificent by a river, its antlers gleaming in the sun. Its beauty almost took his breath away. He paused a moment and in that pause the stag sniffed his presence, spun round and sped into the distance. Hubert gave chase.

All day long the stag tore across the countryside, up hills and down into valleys. All day long the man on his horse tore after him.

At times Hubert would lose sight of the stag and stop, thinking regretfully that he would turn for home; then suddenly once again he would see those antlers, and he would pick up speed again. At times he thought he almost had him, but the animal seemed to gain strength for one more dash for safety and his life.

The shadows were growing longer, the day was drawing to a close; Hubert thought he had lost the trail once more, when he rode out of a thicket into a clearing. There stood the stag, shaking now in fear, exhausted. It could run no more. Hubert drew back his arrow. But he stopped. What was that he saw between the antlers? It looked as though the figure of Jesus on the cross was suspended between the antlers of the deer. He shook himself.

'It must be the evening sun dazzling my eyes,' he thought. 'I must be imagining things.' He drew his arrow again, poised ready to shoot. But no, he saw it again – the figure of Christ hanging on the cross between the antlers.

He could not let fly his arrow. He could not shoot.

He got down from his horse, and knelt in the clearing. Then quietly he turned and led his horse home. That was the end of his hunting. From that time forth he sought to serve his fellow creatures instead of killing them.

Songs

Come and Praise

74 Sad, puzzled eyes
77 The sun burns hot and dry
85 Spirit of peace, come to our waiting world
90 I come like a beggar with a gift in my hand

St. George's Day 23rd April

The material in this assembly could be adapted for a teacher-led assembly.

We have chosen to focus on St. George because this particular saint gives the opportunity to look at the way cultures absorb and assimilate elements from other cultures. Many things which seem intrinsic to the English way of life were once foreign, and St. George is a good example of this. Because this, rather than nationalism, is the focus, we have not included material on St. Patrick, St. Andrew and St. David, especially since this is readily available elsewhere.

Purpose

to help children reflect on the variety of cultures which have contributed to present-day British life

Preparation

In the classroom look at a picture of St. George and the Dragon (e.g. the one by Uccello in the National Gallery) and/or tell the children the bare outlines of the legend: St. George was a knight from Cappadocia (in present-day Turkey) who rescued a maiden from a dragon and became a great hero.

Ask them to make up their own account of the story, working either singly or in groups, explaining to them that while there may once have been a brave Christian called George, the stories about him are legendary. They can now make up their own legend.

Choose an account to dramatize, possibly in comic style, explaining that at fairs in medieval England, groups of mummers went about acting out the story. If you can manage to put the story into rhyming couplets, so much the better!

Look with the children at the fact that St. George is a popular saint in the Middle East, particularly in Syria. Today he is regarded as the patron saint of England, but he wasn't English: the crusaders brought his story back with them and he became very popular in England.

Then use the following information and the children's own ideas to look at things which are taken for granted as being part of English life, to reveal that they had their origins elsewhere.

Sugar

Extracting sugar from cane was known in India around 3000 BCE (Before Common Era). In Sanskrit *sarkara* originally meant sand or gravel (like the texture of sugar). This became *sukkar* in Arabic. Arabs spread its use, and it was found in Spain and southern France by the 8th century – but for a long time it was very expensive.

Columbus took sugar cane plants to the West Indies, where they flourished, and plantations were set up in the West Indies and America, using slave labour. This was when it became cheap and its use became widespread.

Number notation

The number system we now use was adapted by the Arabs from Indian sources in the 9th or 10th century.

In Europe, a Roman system was used until in 1202 an Italian mathematician wrote about the advantages of the Arabic system and the Italian merchants quickly adopted it because it was easier to work with. It spread through Europe, but the scholars were reluctant to use the system, so Roman numerals continued to be used in scholarly works.

Pyjamas

These were loose trousers worn in India. In Urdu *pae* means foot and *jamah* means clothing. Pyjamas were introduced to Britain as nightwear for men in the 1870s. Women began to wear them in the early 20th century.

Bangle

The Hindi word *bangri* means a coloured glass bracelet.

Tea

Tea originated in China about 2700 BCE. It was introduced to Europe in the 18th century. Britain now consumes one fifth of the world's tea crop.

Potatoes
This vegetable was cultivated in South America 1800 years ago. Spaniards introduced it to Europe at the beginning of the 16th century. By the end of the 17th century it was the major crop in Ireland.

Tomatoes
Tomatoes originated in South America and were introduced to Italy in 1544.

Pizza
The word pizza means pie. An encyclopedia published in 1977 has no entry for pizza which shows how new it is, as a common thing, in this country. Discuss tandoori chicken pizzas!

The Royal Family
King George V, in fact from house of Saxe-Coburg-Gotha, adopted the suffix of Windsor in 1917 so as not to sound German. The present Queen decided to use Windsor as her children's surname, rather than her married name of Mountbatten, itself an anglicization of Battenberg.

Christianity
It is worth pointing out to the children that Christianity did not originate in Britain, but began in the Middle East.

Resources

Display on a table a packet of sugar, a picture of the Queen, a pizza, a pair of pyjamas, a bangle, tea, tomatoes, potatoes, etc.

Assembly

First the children present the play of St. George.

Then one child talks briefly about the country of origin of the story and when it came to Britain.

The Leader then tells the children that like St. George, there are many other things which now seem English but originally came from elsewhere. Invite the children to have guesses as to where they came from and then give a brief history of each one.

Prayer/reflection

Ask the children to think of something that comes from another country that they are glad of – either in silence, or making suggestions publicly. Then give a clap for all the good things that come from far away.

Songs

Come and Praise
67 The ink is black, the page is white
69 I belong to a family, the biggest on earth

Baisakhi – Against Injustice

This is best presented as a class assembly.

The Sikh festival of Baisakhi (April 13th) celebrates the formation of the Sikh brotherhood (Khalsa) by the last human Guru, Guru Gobind Singh (see the *REAL Junior Teacher's Handbook* and *A Tapestry of Tales*). A central theme of the festival is the fight against injustice, and for religious freedom. It is the former which is taken up in this assembly.

Purpose

to introduce the children to the festival and help them to reflect on one of its underlying themes: the fight against injustice

Preparation

Tell children the story of the founding of the Khalsa. Then write, as a class or individually, an eyewitness account of the event as a reporter might. Use this as a basis to present the story to the school. Large scale illustrations could be used as the equivalent of camera shots.

Pick up on the themes of injustice and inequality and find out from the children what they consider to be unjust in the world today, on a local and an international level. Collate these into modern news reports.

Discuss with them what they think could be done about these injustices and what they know is being done. Give them the following example of what Sikhs are doing today: when Sikhs were first in Britain they often had difficulty finding places to live, and they were particularly helped by the Irish community, who had themselves been immigrants not long before. Today Sikhs have set up projects to help other immigrants to Britain, especially those who have suffered persecution.

Prepare an interview, as if for radio or television, presenting the points raised in your class discussion.

Assembly

Introduce the assembly by telling the children that Sikhs are celebrating the festival of Baisakhi. Give some background information on Sikhism from Introduction to Sikhism p. 130 *REAL Junior Teacher's Handbook.*

Then present the assembly as a radio or television programme:

1) Report about the founding of the Khalsa (from the archives!)
2) Reports about present-day examples of injustice.
3) Interview the panel about what is being done about this injustice.

Prayer/reflection

Listen to these words from the Guru Granth Sahib:

> After wandering and wandering, O Lord,
> I have come at last to take refuge in Thee.
> Nanak's humble prayer, O God, is –
> Let me be busy in Thy service!
>
> Astapadi, 20; Slok, I

Songs

Come and Praise
71 If I had a hammer
74 Sad, puzzled eyes
88 I was lying in the roadway

Holi

This assembly could be linked to the time of year of the festival (March to April) but it is not essential to do so.

The legends of Krishna's tricks are interpreted in a number of ways by Hindus. Some allegorize the story of the cowherd girls saying that it shows that each of us has to stand before God just as we are, without the pretence that clothes symbolize. The stories affirm the value of fun and laughter, and are extensions of the metaphor of God as lover; a metaphor which is also used in Christian interpretations of the Song of Solomon in the Old Testament and the image of the Church being the bride of Christ.

Purpose

to celebrate jokes, laughter and friendship and to give children an insight into the Hindu festival of Holi

Assembly

Talk to the children about an incident that you remember from your childhood which was hugely enjoyable and sheer fun. Or do your own clowning act for the children (e.g. pretend to bring in a bucket of water and then throw a bucket of bits of coloured paper at the children).

Then go on to tell the children that Hindus tell stories about when their great God Vishnu came to earth as the man Krishna. He came to earth to fight a wicked demon who was terrorizing the earth but while he was on earth he made lots of people laugh and enjoy themselves by playing tricks. One time he crept up to a pool where the girls who looked after cows were having a swim. He stole all their clothes so they had to come and ask for them back. Then they all played and danced together. Krishna played tricks on people, but always with love so that they felt loved by him. You could refer to the story, 'Krishna and the Butter' in *A Tapestry of Tales*, either to recall it if the children already know it, or tell the story here for the first time.

At the festival of Holi, Hindus celebrate that there is fun and laughter in the world despite its many hardships. They tell stories of Krishna's tricks and they clown around. In some places this includes throwing coloured water at each other. They also celebrate the fruitfulness of the earth, eating roasted grain and coconuts, as Holi is the time of the grain harvest in India.

As it is springtime in Britain, you could include an element of celebrating the return of life in spring, and the excitement and energy that some people feel in spring.

You might wish to add that some Christians speak of Jesus as being the clown of God because the stories in the Bible suggest he enjoyed laughter.

Prayer/reflection

Think in silence of a time when you had a lot of fun with a good friend or someone you love. Then give a clap or three cheers for jokes and for the people we share them with.

Song

Come and Praise

98 You shall go out with joy

140 Lead me from death to life (Tell the children that this song is adapted from a prayer that Hindus often use.)

Follow-up

Encourage the children to recount tricks or jokes they have played, where the person who was tricked enjoyed the joke as much as they did. Make a collection of these stories, and help the children to notice (what will almost certainly be the case) that they played them on people that they are fond of or good friends with.

Remembrance Day

The *REAL Infant Assembly Book* offers a simple Remembrance Day service which could be combined with the ideas below for a whole school assembly. The infant assembly focuses on the red poppy; the white dove as a symbol of peace and marking the time at 11 o'clock. Here the focus is the effect of war on children, in particular the Second World War.

This assembly could be prepared either by one class or by several classes, each one picking up one aspect. Alternatively, each aspect could be used as a focus, making a series of assemblies.

Purpose

to share an act of remembrance with the children and to encourage a commitment to peace

Preparation

Research with the children ways in which the Second World War affected the lives of civilians, especially children. One resource is older people in the community who remember the war. Make up a short play with the children, based on the life of someone they interviewed or an imaginary combination of a number of lives. Don't forget to look into the reasons why they had to leave the cities. Have the children write letters home as though they were evacuees. (This links in with History Study Unit Britain since 1930.) Use one of these letters in the Remembrance Day service.

Read older children either the whole or excerpts from *The Diary of Anne Frank*. Help the children to write a brief account of her life.

Read children *Sadako and the Thousand Paper Cranes* by Eleanor Coerr (Hodder and Stoughton, 1977). Alternatively, tell them the following summary of the story:

> On August 6th 1945, American aircraft dropped an atom bomb on the Japanese city of Hiroshima killing 100,000 women, men and children. Many others died later of illnesses which they got as a result of radiation fallout. Among them was Sadako Sasaki who contracted leukemia. In the early stage of her illness a friend brought her a paper origami crane, a custom which is popular among the Japanese as a sign of hope. While she was dying, Sadako folded 644 cranes out of many different coloured scraps of paper brought to her by friends. She made them, at first as a sign of hope that she would overcome the illness and then later as a sign of hope that people would work for peace not war. In 1958 a statue of her holding a paper crane was unveiled in the Hiroshima Peace Park. It commemorated all those children who had died of illnesses contracted as a result of the bomb.

If you have a copy of *Sadako and the Thousand Paper Cranes* you could try making paper cranes with the children, following the instructions in the book – but try it at home first!

Prepare with the children a piece about the cranes. They could also paint a picture of the statue as they imagine it.

Using newspaper cuttings, find out about a war which is currently taking place or is recently over. Look at the effect it is having or has had on the children of the region. Find out if there is any way that the children can contribute to their welfare through organisations like Christian Aid or the Red Cross. Prepare a news report about it.

If you have made the paper cranes you could hang them in the assembly hall.

Set the table with five candles, one larger than the rest.

Assembly

Play quiet music as the children enter.

The leader invites groups of children, in turn, to present a short piece about the effect of the war on the lives of children. The pieces can be based on earlier classroom research. At the end of each section she or one of the children says the words:

> We remember today the children of Great Britain who were hurt or killed by war.
>
> We remember today Anne Frank and other Jewish children who were hurt or killed in the Second World War.
>
> We remember today the children in the countries who were the enemy during the time of the war; the children who were hurt or killed by the war; the children of Germany and Japan.

We remember today the children of wars which still continue.

A child reads the Beatitudes from the gospel of Luke 6 : 20-22.

Then light the last, largest candle with the words:

We remember today all those children who have been hurt or killed by war throughout the ages, and we pray for peace.

Song

Come and Praise

144 Peace is flowing like a river.

Move out quietly.

THE SCHOOL COMMUNITY

Learning about one another is fundamental if a community is to grow as a community, whether it be a church, temple, or school. Assemblies which focus on one member of the community and celebrate them as an individual are one way of doing this. For example an assembly could be built around a 'This Is Your Life' theme for a member of staff, teaching or ancillary (see 'Celebrating the Person' in the *REAL Infant Assembly Book* for another example).

Children's Newsdesk

This is a regular assembly (weekly, fortnightly or monthly) which focuses on news. It also places the school in context as part of a wider community whose concerns are of relevance because we belong to a shared world and have a common humanity. The assembly is modelled on a television news programme.

A slot for news in everyday assemblies is another way of pursuing this objective. This could be followed by a time of silence to remember anyone in need, and applause to celebrate any good news.

Purpose

to help build up the school as a community

Preparation

Write a standard signature tune which is used on each occasion to signal that it is a newstime assembly.

Classes could take turns to be responsible for researching and preparing the assembly. They can collect material from other classes, finding out what they have done as classes and any individual news (e.g. what topics are being studied, outings, children leaving, births of siblings). The children can also set up interviews with members of other classes. It would be up to the children to make the items as interesting as possible, using T.V. news as a model. If the equipment is available, videoing the interviews would be even more effective. Be careful, however, not to let the assembly become too long-winded.

Children can write prayers/reflections about news items.

Set out the front of the hall as though it was a television news studio. Have the television and video ready if interviews have been video-recorded.

Assembly

Children can present the information they have gathered as though it were a television news programme (you might even include up-to-date weather forecasts). Either show on-the-spot reports on video or dramatize them, involving the children from the relevant classes.

At the end have a 'Thought For The Day' time in which children give thanks or remember those in need.

Also, follow with the children one or two central news items for the days preceding the assembly, they could be local or national stories. Help the children prepare reports of them to present to the assembly.

THE NATURAL WORLD

Both the following assemblies encourage children to celebrate the natural world in all its diversity. Celebration must be rooted in valuing, and out of such celebration comes the incentive to care. See also the topic on 'The Living World' in the *REAL Junior Teacher's Handbook.*

The Assisi Pilgrimage

This assembly could be a class one at the end of a topic on journeys or on the natural world. It could also be adapted to be a straight account of the story of the WWF Assisi pilgrimage.

Purpose

to evoke and encourage a commitment to the welfare of the natural world.

Preparation

Weave the following information into a narrative to introduce it to your class:

> In September 1986, representatives from the six major religions in the world and from some smaller religions went on pilgrimage to Assisi, in Italy. They were there at the invitation of His Royal Highness, the Duke of Edinburgh, to mark the 25th Anniversary of the founding of the World Wide Fund for Nature, a conservation body concerned to protect wildlife and its environment. Why Assisi? Because Assisi was the home of St. Francis, the Christian saint, renowned for his love of animals and of all creation (see *A Tapestry of Tales*). What better place could there be for a wildlife celebration?
>
> In the week before the main celebration, groups of pilgrims from many faiths walked across the surrounding hills. They carried big banners celebrating wildlife. They told each other stories from their own traditions about care for the environment. They sang songs about the natural world.

Introduce children to the idea of dramatizing a pilgrimage for the environment. They could proceed around the hall for an assembly. Decide with them which songs they will sing (inviting the rest of the school to join in) and which stories they will tell on the way. They could act out one of them. The stories could focus on St. Francis or be a collection from different faiths of brief tales and readings about animals. (See, too, some of the creation stories, 'The Hare-Mark on the Moon', 'The Monkey Bridge', 'The Thirsty Camel' in *A Tapestry of Tales*. Another good source is *Faith and Nature*, by Martin Palmer, Anne Nash and Ivan Hattingh, obtainable from WWF UK, see below.)

Investigate, with children, the needs of the natural world, given the damage humanity has inflicted on the environment. Help them make banners depicting environmental needs. A collage of brightly coloured material glued onto hessian is simple and effective, or you could sew the material to make the banners last longer. Alternatively, use thick cardboard glued onto sticks.

Find pictures of Assisi and use them to paint a mural for the front of the hall or simply cut out the shape of the basilica.

Find out more about the work of WWF (Panda House, Weyside Park, Catteshall Lane, Godalming, Surrey GU7 1XR). WWF also has more information about the Assisi pilgrimage.

Assembly

Seat the majority of children so that there is plenty of space for others to move round them. Introduce the assembly by briefly mentioning St. Francis and the work of WWF, as well as the Assisi pilgrimage. Then set the class off on pilgrimage round the hall. They could sing as they walk slowly round, inviting other children to gradually join in. The children in the middle of the audience would need to turn to see the procession. They can stop at intervals to tell their stories. (They may have to go round the hall twice).

Finally on arrival in Assisi say the following prayer:

Prayer/reflection

Saint Francis spoke of all creatures as his
brothers and sisters.
Our brothers and sisters in creation, we make a promise to you this day; to you and all creation yet to be.
To every living creature and all that contains and sustains you;
to all that is on earth and to the earth itself;
to all that lives in the waters and to the waters themselves;
to all that flies in the skies and to the sky itself.
We promise to use all our powers to prevent your destruction.

(Adapted from The Rainbow Covenant, *Winchester Creation Harvest Liturgy* (WWF, 1987).

Leave the banners in the hall so the rest of the school can have a closer look.

The Judgement of the Wind

This story has several themes within it and raises a number of issues which are unresolved, despite the wind's judgement. This perhaps is its power as a story – for it should provoke much thought. However, we have focused in the conclusion on the judgement, which links it also to the theme of justice. The tale lends itelf to a dramatic presentation which could be prepared beforehand in class.

Purpose

to stimulate reflection on the problems of justice which arise out of our dependence on other creatures and plants

Assembly

Leader:

Look around you, and think about some of the things that you have done today. How many things in our everyday life come from some other living thing? Look at the wood in this building. We only have that because a tree has been chopped down. Some of us are wearing leather shoes. We have the leather because an animal has been killed. Many people think that it is not right to kill other living things for our benefit. Other people say, Well, that is just the way we are made. We could not live without sometimes killing other living things. Other animals do it, and we are no different.

This story from Ethiopia takes up that idea.

A great snake hid in the forest and preyed upon many living creatures who happened to pass his way. He sometimes went out of the forest and ate the goats and cattle of villagers who lived nearby. At last, a party of hunters went out to destroy him so that their cattle would be safe. With their spears and shields and hunting knives in their hands they looked for the snake where they found signs of him. Hearing them approach, he fled into a cotton field where a farmer was working.

The farmer was about to drop his tools and run away, but the snake said:

'Brother, enemies are following me to kill me. Hide me so that I shan't die.'

The farmer thought for a moment and then said:

'Though you have a bad reputation, one must have sympathy for the hunted.'

And he hid the snake in a large pile of cotton standing in his field. When the hunters came along they asked:

'Have you seen the serpent that kills our cattle?'

'I have not seen him,' the farmer replied, and the hunters went on.

The snake came out from under the cotton.

'They are gone,' the farmer said. 'You are safe'.

But the snake did not go away. He took hold of the farmer.

'What are you doing?' the farmer asked.

'I am hungry,' the snake said. 'I shall have to eat you.'

'What? I save your life and then you wish to destroy mine?'

'I am hungry,' the snake replied. 'I have no choice.'

'You are ungrateful,' the farmer said.

'I am hungry,' the snake said.

'Since it is like this, let us have our case judged,' the farmer said.

'Very well. Let the tree judge us.'

So they went before the huge sycamore tree, which grew at the side of the road. Each of them stated his case, while the tree listened.

Then the tree said to the farmer:

'I stand here at the edge of the road and give shade. Tired travellers come and sit in my shade to rest. And then, when they have finished, they cut off my branches to make axe handles and ploughs. Man is ungrateful for the good I do him. Therefore, since it is this way, I cannot judge in your favour. The snake is entitled to eat you.'

The snake and the man went then to the river, and again they told their story. The river listened, and then it said to the farmer:

'I flow here between my banks and provide man with water. Without me, man would suffer; he would not have enough to drink. In the dry season when there are no rains, man comes and digs holes in my bed to find water for himself and his cattle. But when heavy rains come I am filled to the brink. I cannot hold so much water, and I overflow onto man's fields. Then man becomes angry. He comes to me and curses me and throws stones at me. He forgets the good I do him. I have no use for man. Therefore, since this is man's nature, I cannot judge in your favour. The snake may eat you.'

The snake and the man went to the grass, and once more they told their story. The grass listened, and then it said to the farmer:

'I grow here in the valley and provide food for man's cattle. I give myself to man to make roofs for his houses, and to make baskets for his kitchen. But then man puts the torch to me when I am old, and burns me. And after that he ploughs me under and plants grain in my place, and wherever I grow among the grain he digs me out and kills me. Man is not good. Therefore, I cannot judge in your favour. The snake may eat you.'

The snake took hold of the farmer and they went away from the grass.

'The judgement is very cruel,' the farmer said.

But on the road they met the wind. And though he had no hope, the farmer once more told his story. The wind listened and then it said:

'All things live according to their nature. The grass grows to live and man burns it to live. The river flows to live, and it overflows its banks because that is its nature; it cannot help it. And man grieves when his planted fields are flooded, for they are his life. The tree cherished its branches for they are its beauty and the snake eats whatever it finds, for that, too, is his nature. So you see one cannot blame the tree, the grass, and the river for their judgement, nor can one blame the snake for his hunger.'

The farmer became even more sad, for he saw no way out for him. But the wind went on:

'So this is not a matter for judgement at all, but for all things acting according to their nature. Therefore, let us dance and sing in thanks because all things are as they are.'

And the wind gave the farmer a drum to play, and he gave the snake a drum to play also. In order to hold his drum the snake had to let go of the farmer.

'As your nature is to eat man, eat man,' the wind sang to the snake.

The wind turned to the farmer:

'As your nature is not to be eaten, do not be eaten!' it sang.

'Amen!' the farmer replied with feeling. And as the snake was no longer holding him, he threw down his drum and fled safely to his village.

From *The Fire on the Mountain* by H. Courlander (Holt, Rhinehart and Winston, 1950)

Note: at the author's request, we have retained his use of the word 'man' to mean all humanity.

Prayer/reflection

The wind said, 'Therefore, let us dance and sing in thanks because all things are as they are.' We give thanks for the variety of living things in the world. Let us be people who respect other living things and value them for what they are.

A Christian called Jacob Boehme wrote this prayer:

> For this I thank You, that You have created me to Your image, and placed Your wonders under my hands so that I may know them and rejoice in the works of Your creation.
>
> I pray to You, eternal God, give me understanding and wisdom that I might not misuse Your creation but use it only for my needs, for the good of my neighbour, myself (and my family). Give me gratitude for all Your gifts, so that my reason does not say: 'This is mine. I have purchased it. I will possess it alone.'

Jacob Boehme, *The Way to Christ* (SPCK Classics of Western Spirituality series, 1978) trans. Peter C. Erb. Quoted from *Faith and Nature*, Palmer, Nash and Hattingh (WWF/Rider, 1987).

Songs

Come and Praise

73 When your Father made the world

76 God in his love for us lent us this planet

Follow-up

Look at an aspect of the local area, e.g. local park, river, disused railway cutting. Discuss what nature offers to humanity. How do the children think humanity has treated it in return?

OUR LOCAL AREA

The *REAL Junior Teacher's Handbook* has a topic on the local area. Here are two ways of following up class work in this topic.

A Guide

This is a class assembly which builds on work done in 'The Local Area' topic in the *REAL Junior Teacher's Handbook*. This assembly is designed to be a celebration of the local community.

Purpose

to present to children from another class the results of research and to invite them to affirm the importance of the local community

Preparation

Invite a local community representative into the school (e.g. a councillor, M.P., mayor, religious leader) or the librarian. Have a copy of the guide to the local area you have made on display.

Assembly

One child introduces the book for the local area. Other children pretend to be various people who might use the book, e.g. 'I have just moved into the area and I am not feeling well. Can your book tell me where to find a doctor?'

Another child replies, reporting the information that is in the book.

Weave into this presentation the fact that some facilities are not recorded in the book because as far as the children could find out these were not available locally.

Then in a small ceremony present the book to the local community representative.

Leader:

> Let us give a big cheer for our community; for all the people young and old, rich and poor, some who are well, others who have to cope with illness or disability; for those who live here and for those who come to work here.

Song

Come and Praise

19 He's got the whole world (adapting the words to include the local community)

Celebration of a Local Religious Building

This assembly is based on work in the *REAL Junior Teacher's Handbook* topic 'A Place of Worship'. An alternative assembly, based on the same work, is to present a pageant of the history of the building, drawing out what has remained constant and what has changed, over the years.

Purpose

to share with the rest of the school what the children have learnt from visiting the religious building and to invite them to begin to value their role in the community

Preparation

Make symbols of various features of the religious building you have studied, and pin them up round the assembly room. These could include architectural features, such as a baptismal font (church), minbar (mosque), or something to symbolize an activity, such as scripture classes. Prepare short introductions to each one, preferably in dramatic form.

Assembly

The child leader of the assembly invites the class to do an imaginary tour of the religious building as he or she moves from one symbol to another, as though touring the building. At each symbol children stationed there can explain it in a short dramatic form, for example, by acting out the activity that takes place there.

Prayer/reflection

Let us give thanks for all that [name the religious building] has contributed to our community.

Song

If possible, learn some music that is used in the religious building you have studied, or see if you can borrow some appropriate, recorded music.

FRIENDSHIP

In the topic called 'Friends' in the *REAL Junior Teacher's Handbook* some of the problems of friendship are explored, as well as the value. Here we give two stories which celebrate the value of friendship.

The Book of Life

This story clearly links with the Christian idea, paralleled in other faiths, that one should be seeking true treasures not worldly ones of gold and silver.

Purpose

to reflect on things that are precious although of no monetary value

Assembly

Leader:

What does it mean to be very rich? Listen to the story and find out one answer.

A Jewish legend tells how, in the days of Solomon, King of Israel, a shepherd lived in the hills north of Jerusalem. Word spread among the people that he had some rare and precious parchments hidden in a secret cave. In those days parchments were rare. The King had some, and the priests had some, but no ordinary person owned parchment. So it is not surprising that when the King heard about this shepherd he sent a messenger to fetch him to appear before the King.

'Tell him to bring his rare scrolls with him,' said the King, 'so that the scholars of Jerusalem may study them.'

Within a fortnight the shepherd arrived, with a heavy box on his head. He put this down before the King, took out his parchments and began to spread them out one by one.

'Why, there is nothing on them!' exclaimed the Kings scholars. 'Nothing but the names of a few fishermen, shepherds, farmers, travelling merchants, and ordinary people like that!'

'Well, to be sure, O King,' replied the shepherd. 'That is all they are, to you and to everybody else. But to me each of them is a page in my life. When I win a friend, I set a page for him in my book of life, and I try to fill it with words of kindness and with deeds of friendship. And when my friend dies or deserts me, a page is torn from my life.'

'You have here a great treasure indeed, said the wise King Solomon, I would gladly give up many of my treasure rooms and storehouses full of good things for a few of your pages of friendship.'

Adapted from *Lost Legends of Israel*, Dagobert D. Runes, New York, 1961

Prayer/reflection

Do not store up treasures for yourselves on earth, where moths and woodworms destroy them and thieves can break in and steal. But store up treasures for yourselves in heaven, where neither moth nor woodworms destroy them and thieves cannot break in and steal. For where your treasure is, there will your heart be also. (Matthew 6:19–22)

Songs

Alleluya

38 With a little help from my friends

Come and Praise

57 Think of all the things we lose

87 (alternative words) Give us friends, Lord, for each day

Follow-up

Ask the children to make a treasure box out of paper and then slip into it symbols representing what one should truly treasure in life.

Three Friends

This assembly also links with 'Remembrance Day' on p. 12.

Purpose

to celebrate long-lasting friendships

Preparation

Have a candle ready, and, if possible, a map of the world to point to as you tell the story. Find also pictures of Vienna and Sydney.

Assembly

Introduce this true story by telling the children about someone you have known for a long time. Comment that some friendships only last a short time but are good while they last. Others last much longer.

Katie, Trudie and Liesel were friends at school. They lived in the same district of the city of Vienna. When they were little they played games in the street together, ball games, singing games and games with hoops, as children did in those days and still do. When they were teenagers they sat in each other's rooms and laughed and giggled and talked about their friends and worried about their homework as teenagers did then and still do. There was a war on, a great and terrible war, but it scarcely touched their lives.

They grew up. Katie and Trudie became secretaries and worked for businesses in the city. Liesel studied to be a child psychologist so she could help small children. But they stayed friends. They often met for lunch in the park, or went out in the evenings.

But then came rumours of the possibility of another war. Adolf Hitler had become leader of the German people. He gave them pride again to be Germans after their defeat in the first war. His troops marched into Austria. Many of the Austrians were pleased. They lined the streets to welcome the soldiers.

But some Austrians were very frightened, among them Katie, Trudie and Liesel, for they were Jews. They knew that in Germany Hitler's secret police had bombed the synagogues where the Jews prayed. They knew that Jewish doctors, businesspeople, lawyers and teachers had been forced out of their work, and without work they had no money to buy things to eat. They knew too, that many Jewish people had disappeared. They had been packed together like sardines on a train and sent into the unknown. The women wondered what would happen to them, and they soon realised what danger they were in.

Some British people saw that the Jews in Austria and Germany were in great peril and they asked the British government for help to bring them to Britain. But there was little help. They smuggled some Jews out of the country by hiding them in the boot of their cars, or guiding them across mountain tracks to safety. They got jobs for others by persuading families in Britain to take on cooks and housekeepers. And this is what happened to Katie, Trudie and Liesel. They were offered jobs in England. At first they didn't want to go. They didn't want to leave their families but their families urged them to go. 'Its your only hope,' they said. 'You must take it.'

It was hard being a cook when you couldn't cook and a housekeeper when you had always hated housework. Three British families ate some strange meals that winter! The three women found it hard to have to speak English, struggling to remember the English they had learnt in school. They were always glad when it was their day off, and they could meet and chatter away in German.

After a few months the opportunity came to go to start a new life in Sydney, Australia. There Katie and Liesel married Australians and Liesel started a nursery for small children. Trudie became a housekeeper to a Hungarian Jewish refugee. She lived on a small chicken farm, thirty miles out of Sydney with no proper toilet. It was a very different life to life in Vienna. But still Trudie kept in touch with her two friends.

For nearly seven years they heard nothing of their families because war had broken out in Europe. Many countries around the world, including Britain and Australia, had joined together to drive out Hitler. Then in 1945 war ended. Hitler had been defeated and news began to trickle through of what had happened. All Liesel's family had died. Katie's brothers had both escaped but her parents had died in one of Hitler's camps. One of Trudie's brothers had survived the terrible concentration camps where the Jews were sent, but her sister, another brother and her parents had all perished. The friendship between the three women became even more important.

And the three friends grew old together. Trudie made clothes for Liesel and Katie's children and grandchildren. They had lunch together most weeks, talking away in German as they had done since they were small girls together. In 1988 Liesel died and in 1989 Katie died. It had been a friendship which had lasted seventy years, and in some ways even longer, for when this story was written in 1991, Trudie lived in an old people's home and would go to visit Katie's daughter for Sunday dinner.

Prayer/reflection

Light a candle, and spend a short time in silence in memory of all those who have had to flee their homes because of war.

Let's give a big clap for friendships which could not be broken by war.

Follow-up

Talk with the children about people growing old together. Do they know any adults who have been friends since childhood? Discuss with them the reasons why people sometimes lose touch with friends. Ask them to draw a picture of themselves and a close friend as very old people.

Some of the children in your class may have left their city of birth, and there are some refugee children in Britain, invite children to talk or write about such changes in their lives. Consider the plight of refugees from hunger as well as war in a geography topic.

Initiate a topic on what happened in Britain during the war, and look particularly at evacuees.

Read *The Diary of Anne Frank* or *Hitler Stole Pink Rabbit* by Judith Kerr to a top junior class.

FOOD

This links with the topic Food in the *REAL Junior Teacher's Handbook*.

Use the same model for an assembly on sweets but instead use the blessing:

> You are blessed, Lord our God, the sovereign of the world, by whose word everything came into being.

Bread

Purpose
to share (literally!) the results of the children's studies with the rest of the school

Preparation
Children should bake enough bread for each child in school to have a small piece. (This is not as much as it might at first sound – a standard small loaf will make 400 pieces, and rolls can be divided at least into eight.) Prepare the children to mime the different processes in breadmaking, following a recipe they have used in class.

Assembly
A child introduces the topic of bread and then reads out the recipe with children miming each stage.

One child talks about bread being a symbol both of sustenance and of sharing (see *REAL Junior Teacher's Handbook*). The sharing of bread is a common symbol for the sharing of friendship and hospitality. It is one aspect of the Christian Communion service.

Children cut up the bread and one says:

> People of the Jewish faith say these words before they eat bread.
>
> You are blessed, Lord our God, the sovereign of the world, who brings forth bread from the earth.

Then children pass round the baskets of bread so that every child can have a piece.

Song
Come and Praise

139 Now the harvest is all gathered

MESSAGES WITHOUT WORDS

The chapter in the *REAL Junior Teacher's Handbook* specifically develops the religious aspects of this theme. Assembly is a good time to draw children's attention to how much can be, and often is, expressed without words.

Plays Without Words

This assembly links with the topic on 'Messages Without Words' in the *REAL Junior Teacher's Handbook*.

Purpose

to show others one aspect of the topic they have been studying in class

Preparation

Prepare with the children two or three very short plays (lasting for two to three minutes) which use no words but rely on music, artefacts, art and gesture to convey their meaning. Make sure a range of emotions is expressed in the plays and that they include the theme of gifts. One play could have an explicitly religious context.

Assembly

One child introduces the topic and asks the school to try to follow the plays.

Act out the plays.

One child identifies for the audience the range of non-verbal communications on which the plays depended.

Prayer/reflection

Help us to pay attention to everything that tells us something:
to what we see
to what we hear
to what we smell
to what we feel
to what we taste.
Let us understand the messages, not just the words.

Song

Come and Praise
11 For the beauty of the earth

JUSTICE

Justice is an important theme in most faiths, including Christianity. It was a major preoccupation of the Old Testament prophets in whose tradition Jesus followed. These assemblies raise the question of what is justice, as well as ways of achieving it.

Also see the assembly 'The Judgement of the Wind', p. 58, and the topic on 'Rules and Justice' in the *REAL Junior Teacher's Handbook*.

The Lion and the Hermit

This story is essentially about justice although it does also have within it the Utopian dream of animals being at peace with one another.

Purpose
to invite reflection on a story which has many worthwhile themes in it

Assembly
There are many stories from different parts of the world about people or animals being misjudged and accused of something they have not done. This story is told in Greek Orthodox churches.

Gerasimos was a hermit who lived by the Jordan river. He wanted to be alone with God and with the beautiful things that God had created, and he wanted to be far away from cities and noise and the many unimportant things that people made a fuss about. By day and by night Gerasimos prayed and meditated silently, and in his heart sang silent hymns of praise to God. His only companions were a disciple who wanted to learn how to know God as Gerasimos did, and a donkey.

Gerasimos was so quiet and so holy that eventually even the wild beasts of the desert knew that he was a saint, and became tame and gentle in his presence.

One day a great lion came out of the desert and approached Gerasimos's hut. The lion came up to Gerasimos, bowed its head and held out a huge paw. It was indicating that it wanted to stay with Gerasimos and serve him as the donkey and the disciple did.

So the lion joined the little community that lived by the Jordan river, and although the lion could easily have eaten both the men and the donkey, they all lived together in perfect peace and harmony.

One of the lion's tasks was to go with the donkey when it went looking for fodder, and guard it from the other wild beasts of the desert. One hot day when the lion and the donkey were out together as usual, the lion lay down in the shade of a tree while the donkey grazed, and before long, the lion was asleep.

While he slept, some merchants passed by. They saw the donkey apparently all alone and unguarded in the desert, and they put a rope around its neck and took it away with them.

When the lion awoke, he was very upset to find the donkey gone. He knew he should not have slept and left the donkey unguarded. He searched everywhere, but eventually had to return to the hermit's hut without the donkey.

When Gerasimos and his disciple saw the lion coming back without the donkey, they both assumed that the obvious thing had happened.

'The lion must have eaten the donkey,' said the disciple. 'How shall we punish him?'

'We shall make him do the work that the donkey used to do,' said Gerasimos. 'He must carry water whenever we need it.'

The lion was a proud beast, and carrying water was a very lowly and menial task. But the lion, although he could have killed Gerasimos and his disciple with one blow of his paw, obeyed them, and whenever water was needed, the disciple led him down to the river, filled the big water jugs, and loaded them on the lion's back. The lion knew that he was not guilty of eating the donkey, but he knew he should not have slept while he was guarding him.

After some time, the merchants finished their business and returned home the same way they had come. The lion's sharp eyes soon spotted the travellers, and with them the hermit's donkey. With a loud roar, he rushed at the merchants, and sent them scurrying away across the desert. With his teeth he took hold of the donkey's bridle and led him back to Gerasimos's house.

When Gerasimos saw the lion standing there with the donkey, he knew that he had treated him unjustly all those months. He called his disciple, and said,

'Look, here is our donkey. The lion did not eat him, and yet we punished him. Now we must make amends for punishing him so unjustly.' Then he turned to the lion.

'You have served us well and faithfully, even when we were unjust to you. Now it is time for you to return to your home in the desert. You are free. Go, my dear friend, with my blessing.'

The lion bowed his great head before the saint whom he had loved and served so long. Then he turned and vanished into the desert.

But back in the desert, far away from the river and his old companions, the lion became lonely. So every week he went back for a visit. Every time it was a happy reunion of man and beast, as the two men and two animals greeted each other.

Until one day the lion came for his weekly visit and there were only two friends to greet him, the disciple and the donkey. Gerasimos had died. With his head bent in sorrow, the lion showed that he wanted to see the saint's grave. The disciple led the lion to the place where Gerasimos was buried. A small wooden cross marked the place. The lion looked at the grave, then he lay down in the same place and died. The lion could not live without the saint who had loved God and all his creatures so much.

Adapted from Eva C. Topping, *Sacred Stories from Byzantium*, HCO Press, Brookline, Mass., U.S.A.

Prayer/reflection

In Shakespeare's play, *Hamlet*, a father gives this advice to his son who is about to leave home for the first time:

> Give every man thy ear, but few thy voice;
> Take each man's censure, but reserve thy judgement.

The book of Ecclesiastes, in the Bible, says the same thing in a different way:

> Do not be hasty with your resentment, for resentment is found in the heart of fools. (Eccl. 7:9–10)

Think about a time when someone misjudged you, or when you were too quick to blame another person.

Songs

Come and Praise

68 Kum bah ya (Suggest that as the children sing it they think about people who have been falsely accused)
71 If I had a hammer

Follow-up

Children can write a story set at home or school about someone making a quick judgement. It can be either fictional or about an actual time when they have either misjudged someone or been misjudged themselves.

Read the children Dick King-Smith's novel *The Sheep-pig* which picks up a similar theme.

The Goats Who Killed the Leopard

Purpose
to reflect on one reason why we do not always act justly

Assembly
Leader:

Once a leopard cub wandered away from his home into the grasslands where the elephant herds grazed. He was too young to know the danger. While the elephants grazed one of them stepped upon the leopard cub by accident, and killed him. Other leopards found the body of the cub soon after, and they rushed to his father to tell him of the tragedy.

'Your son is dead!' they told him. 'We found him in the valley!'

The father leopard was overcome with grief.

'Ah, who has killed him? Tell me, so that I can avenge his death!'

'The elephants have killed him,' the other leopards said.

'What? The elephants?' the father leopard said with surprise in his voice.

'Yes, the elephants,' they repeated.

He thought for a minute.

'No, it is not the elephants. It is the goats who have killed him. Yes, the goats, it is they who have done this thing to me!'

So the father leopard went out in a fit of terrible rage and found a herd of goats grazing in the hills, and he slaughtered many of them in revenge.

And even now, when a man is wronged by someone stronger than himself, he often avenges himself upon someone who is weaker than himself.

From *The Fire on the Mountain* by H. Courlander (Holt, Rhinehart and Winston, 1950)

Note: At the request of the author we have retained his use of the word 'man' to mean all humanity.

Leader:

Think about this story a minute and think about yourself.

Have you ever come home from school tired and cross because someone has teased you, or because you've been in trouble and you thought it was unfair? And have you then teased your little brother or sister or kicked the cat? Many people might do this, but do you think it is fair?

Prayer/reflection
When we have been hurt,
May we learn not to hurt another in return.

When someone has wronged us,
May we learn not to wrong someone else.

Anger and hurt and wrongdoing can spread like ripples in a pool.
May we learn to still the ripples and not pass them on.

Songs
Come and Praise
140 Lead me from death to life
142 I'm gonna lay down my sword and shield
147 Make me a channel of your peace

Follow-up
Ask the children to make up their own version of the story. It is one which occurs in a number of guises in different traditions.

Can Gold Turn into Brass?

Purpose

to explore whether 'two wrongs make a right'

Assembly

Once upon a time in Burma, the laws of the country were not written down as they are now, but people learned how to judge difficult cases by telling stories. This is one of many stories about Princess Learned-in-the-Law, who gave wise judgements for her people.

In a forest there once lived a hermit. He lived all alone, eating fruit and vegetables, and people thought of him as a very holy man. However, he did possess a pot of gold, and he lived in fear in case the people of the nearby village should find out that he still possessed worldly riches.

One day a villager and his wife came to him with their only son, who was known as Master Moon.

'My Lord,' said the villager, 'I have a request to make. Will you accept our son as your pupil, and let him be your servant and help you both day and night?'

The hermit agreed, and as time went by, he became quite friendly with the villager as the man came and went on visits to his son. Eventually the hermit came to trust the villager so much that he told him about the pot of gold, and his fear that someone would discover it.

'Don't worry, my Lord Hermit,' said the villager. 'Let me take it away and keep it safe until you want it again. No-one will know that it really belongs to you.'

The hermit was very relieved, and gave the gold to the villager. He settled down to his usual ways feeling that a load had been taken off his mind.

But a few weeks later, the villager came to him looking very worried.

'What is the matter?' asked the hermit.

'My lord, look at this,' said the villager, showing him the pot. 'Your gold has turned to brass!'

The hermit knew that the villager had stolen his gold, but he knew that it would be no good telling anyone, as no-one would believe that he had owned gold. So he just took the pot and said nothing. But in the next few days he thought up a plan.

He began to tame a young monkey from the forest. He gave it bananas and sugar-cane so that it would come running whenever the hermit called out the name Master Moon. Now the hermit's plan was ready. One day when he knew that the villager would come to visit his son Master Moon, he took the boy to a place far away in the forest. He told him to climb to the top of a tall tree and not come down until the hermit came back.

Then he went back to his house and waited for the villager. When the man arrived, the hermit greeted him with sorrow.

'Why are you sitting alone?' the villager asked. 'And where is my son Master Moon?'

'Oh dear,' sighed the hermit. 'I am afraid you are going to be upset by what you see.' Then he called out,

'Master Moon! Master Moon! Come here, your father has come to visit!'

At once the little monkey came running out of the trees.

'You are a cheat!' shouted the villager. 'You are lying! How can a boy turn into a monkey?'

'O villager,' said the hermit calmly, 'if gold can turn into brass, then surely a boy can turn into a monkey.'

Eventually the case came before Princess Learned-in-the-Law. She couldn't help smiling when she heard what each one had to say, and this was the judgement she gave:

'Everyone is responsible for the safety of something that is entrusted to them. The gold was entrusted to the villager, and the boy was entrusted to the hermit. The villager must return the gold, and the hermit must return the boy. If you both do this, I will ask the king to pardon you both, although you have both proved that you are cheats by insisting that gold can turn into brass and a boy can turn into a monkey.'

Adapted from *Burmese Law Tales* (OUP) by Maung Htin Aung.

Prayer/reflection

Think about the story in silence. Have you ever tried to cheat someone who cheated you? How do you think the other person felt?

Follow-up

Discuss with the children whether it is right to cheat someone who has cheated you.

What is the Smell Worth?

There are links here with the theme of money in the *REAL Junior Teacher's Handbook*.

In a world where it sometimes seems that everything is to be valued according to its marketable rate, this raises the issue that many things of value cannot and should not be bought and sold.

Assembly

Leader:

> A poor traveller sat under a tree in Burma, eating the simple meal which he had brought with him. All he had was some boiled rice and a few cooked vegetables. It was the cool season, when many people choose to travel, so at the side of the road there were several stalls selling cooked food for the more wealthy travellers. The poor traveller had sat down just to the south of a stall where a woman was selling fried fish. She watched the traveller carefully, and when he had finished eating, she said to him,
>
> 'Give me a silver coin for the fried fish.'
>
> 'But I haven't eaten any of your fried fish!' protested the traveller.
>
> 'Don't try to cheat me!' said the woman. 'Everyone can see that you have been sitting near my stall and enjoying the smell from my fried fish. Your rice and vegetables wouldn't have tasted so good without the smell of my fish!'
>
> A crowd soon gathered to listen to the argument. They felt sympathy for the traveller, but they had to admit that the wind was blowing from the north, and had definitely carried the smell of the fish to where the traveller was sitting. And they all agreed that a good smell was one of the most enjoyable things about a meal. Without a good smell, nothing tastes so good.
>
> Eventually the case came before Princess Learned-in-the-Law. Everyone trusted her judgement for she was wise in all things. She heard all the evidence, and then said:
>
> 'It is clear that the traveller did smell the fish, and did get some benefit from it. So, clearly, he must pay for it. But what is the price of the smell of fried fish? The woman says that fried fish sells for a silver coin for a plateful. So now the woman and the traveller must go outside into the sunlight. The traveller must hold out a silver coin, and the woman is entitled to the shadow cast by the coin. For if the price of a plate of fried fish is a silver coin, then the price of the *smell* of a plate of fish is the shadow of a silver coin.'

Adapted from *Burmese Law Tales* (OUP) by Maung Htin Aung.

Prayer/reading

Here is a saying of Jesus who also knew the value of things that cannot be bought and sold:

> Do not store up treasures for yourselves on earth, where moths and woodworms destroy them and thieves can break in and steal. But store up treasures for yourselves in heaven, where neither moth nor woodworms destroy them and thieves cannot break in and steal. For where your treasure is, there will your heart be also.

Matthew 6:19–22

Song

Come and Praise

59 I'll bring to you the best gift I can offer

CHANGE

At the heart of the Christian gospel is the hope that people and relationships can change for the better. Life is not determined and fatalistic. This theme is explored as part of the topic on 'Change' in the *REAL Junior Teacher's Handbook* where there are also stories which can be used in assemblies on this theme (St. Francis of Assisi, St. Paul, the Buddha, and others). The assemblies 'Nathan and David' and 'Icons' under the title 'Mirrors' could also be used as part of a series on change as could the story of 'St. Hubert' in the 'Times and Seasons' assemblies.

These two stories look at some of the ways that change can come about.

A Change of Heart

Purpose
to look at one way that change can come about in the way people treat each other

Assembly
Leader:

Hulan loathed her mother-in-law. Oh, how she hated her! She hated her so much that she went to the wise woman who lived deep in the middle of the woods and she said,

'Wise woman, give me a poison to kill my mother-in-law. All day long she sits in the corner of our tiny cottage and she complains. She complains about the pain in her back. She complains about the bunions on her feet. She complains about her aching head but most of all she complains about me. The food I cook is too salty, or it is too sweet. The pillows on the bed are not comfortable enough. The clothes are never clean enough and of course I don't look after her son properly. Oh no, not at all, not like she did when she was fit and well. I am fed up with her screeching at me. I am fed up with her moans. I am fed up with her nagging. I can stand it no longer. Please just give me something that will send her into the next life!'

'Well now,' replied the wise woman. 'I think I have just the thing to meet your need. It is a magic ointment. You must rub it gently into her back twice a day. Remember, it must be done gently, very gently. It won't do to do it roughly. She musn't get suspicious. And remember too that it won't work in a hurry. It will take time, as these things do. Come back to me in one month.'

For a month Hulan rubbed the ointment into her mother-in-law's back. Softly and firmly Hulan soothed the cream into the tired body, trying her hardest not to let her anger and resentment seep through her fingers. At first the old woman was reluctant to let her near. At first she wriggled and squirmed. At first she complained as usual. At last she became still and quiet and the two women, each one with their own thoughts, were together in sildmce.

After a month Hulan returned to the wise woman.

'It hasn't worked yet,' she said. 'It's not been as bad as I thought touching the old one, but I wish its magic would hurry up.'

'I told you it would take time,' replied the wise woman. 'Now take another jar. I've heard you have a beautiful voice. Perhaps if you sing softly and sweetly while you rub in the ointment, it will speed up the magic.'

A month passed and again Hulan hurried through the woods to visit the wise woman.

'Still hasn't worked,' she sighed. 'Mind you, I've quite enjoyed the singing. It's made me sing much more. I had forgotten how much I used to like it. And it's cheered the old woman up a bit.

She even joins in sometimes. Makes it all a bit more bearable. Give me another jar then, please. I hope this one works. It is getting a bit expensive for me.'

'Time, time, everything takes time,' responded the wise woman. 'You'll need to be patient. Try making conversation with the old woman, that sometimes makes it work faster. Ask her about her night's sleep, ask about her day, ask her about your husband, her son, when he was younger. Yes, try that. I think that will help.'

Hulan returned home wondering whether her mother-in-law would talk, wondering if she could stand to listen.

A year passed. Hulan did not go back to the wise woman, but one day she met her by chance in another town.

'You did not return,' said the wise woman. 'Did my magic ointment work at last?'

'Oh no!' laughed Hulan scornfully. 'It didn't work. It didn't work at all. In fact my mother-in-law seemed to grow stronger and healthier because of it! But do you know, I don't really mind. I've got very fond of the old woman. Her stories of her youth are quite interesting, and often she's bothered about what I am doing. She wants to hear about the life in the town and what's going on. No, we have become good friends. I shall be sorry when she dies. No, your magic ointment didn't work at all . . . fortunately!'

As they bid each other farewell and went their separate ways the wise woman chuckled to herself. For she knew that her magic potion had worked very well. It had worked very well indeed.

Prayer/reflection

Stop and think about the story. In what way had the magic worked?

Song

Come and Praise
88 I was lying in the roadway

Follow-up

Talk about why old people are sometimes grumpy and complaining. What could children learn from old people?

One Thousand Deaths

This could also fit with the theme 'People who are remembered'.

Purpose
to look at a sudden change of heart and its results

Assembly
One of the greatest wonders of the world is the Great Wall of China, built over two thousand years ago. It stretches for over two thousand kilometres across northern China, and is nine metres high. It is so big that it can be seen from space. This wall has inspired many stories and legends. This is one of them.

Long ago there lived a powerful and wicked Emperor of China. His soldiers were feared by both his enemies and his own people. The Emperor took the wealth of the land and spent it on building magnificent palaces. He taxed the people so much they were driven into poverty, while he lived in luxury. Those who could not pay his taxes were made to work for no pay at all. He made them build the Great Wall of China, designed to keep out China's enemies.

One day a fortune-teller came to see the Emperor. 'My Lord,' the fortune-teller said. 'Your great wall will fall to the enemy unless you do as I say. You must bury the bodies of a thousand victims in the walls. Their spirits will then protect the wall.'

Immediately the Emperor summoned his wisest advisors and told them of the fortune-teller's words. They were horrified. They begged the Emperor not to kill so many innocent people. But he would not listen, until at last the oldest advisor spoke.

'My Lord. We cannot waste a thousand men. But what if we were to bury one man who is a thousand strong?'

'Explain what you mean,' the Emperor demanded.

'Bury someone called Mr. Tsien – that will do the trick.'

Everyone smiled, for in Chinese 'Tsien' means one thousand and is quite a common surname. The Emperor agreed and the advisers heaved a sigh of relief. No one gave a moment's thought to the poor innocent Mr. Tsien or his family.

A Mr. Tsien was soon found and despite the piteous pleas of his wife and children, he was dragged off to the Emperor's prison and preparations were made for his death the next day.

That night the Emperor sat upon his throne in his vast, beautiful throne room in the Palace. He was pleased with himself: powerful, feared, wealthy and strong. He knew his name would be remembered for ever.

Suddenly the calm of the night was shattered by a thunderous blow on the main door of the throne room. The Emperor sat upright and soldiers ran forward, swords at the ready.

'Who dares to disturb me?' bellowed the Emperor. But there came no answer. 'Who dares to disturb me?' the Emperor shouted again.

At that moment the great doors bulged and collapsed in a pile of dust and rusty iron. As the dust settled, a terrifying figure stood framed by the doorway. As he moved slowly forward the Emperor could see he was dressed as an Emperor of old. Soldiers rushed forward to seize him. But no sooner had they drawn near than their armour rusted away and their flesh melted and they fell as skeletons to the ground. As the horrified Emperor watched, the figure advanced slowly down the length of the room. As he passed, pillars rotted, the walls collapsed and the roof caved in.

Trembling from head to toe, the Emperor was rooted to his throne as the figure drew nearer. Finally, in a voice weak with fear, the Emperor asked,

'Who are you?'

The strange figure spoke at last.

'I am Yao the Emperor, known as Yao the Good. I have returned from the dead to warn you. See – your palace is a ruin; your soldiers just bones. So it will be in a hundred years' time. How then will people remember you? As a wicked, grasping, cruel Emperor. You try to build monuments to yourself in wood and gold, stone and jewels. But the only true monument to you will be how people remember you. Will you be remembered for your cruelty – or for your mercy and compassion? Look at the dust of the future and tremble.'

So saying, Yao reached forward and touched the throne. Instantly the throne crumbled, throwing the Emperor onto the ground. When he looked up again, Yao was gone – and the Emperor awoke. That night he did not sleep, but walked the corridors of his palace thinking.

The next morning he arrived at the great square where the execution of innocent Mr. Tsien was to take place. Just as the executioner prepared to kill Tsien, the Emperor shouted.

'No! No death! No wall can keep an enemy out, but the love of the people will defend our land. Free the man!'

The crowd roared their approval, surprised at this change of heart. They were even more astonished when he ordered all taxes to be cut to just a tenth of what they had been. They were left speechless when he offered to give back land and money taken unjustly from people.

When the enemy did attack, the people rose to defend their beloved land and Emperor. And it is said that people did remember the Emperor for hundreds of years afterwards, telling their children and their children's children about him.

Prayer/reflection

Ask the children to think silently, 'How would I like to be remembered?'

Songs

Come and Praise

50 When a knight won his spurs

71 If I had a hammer

Follow-up

Children can write stories about 'How I changed my mind'. Encourage the children to write about their memories of a friend or how they would remember them.

DREAMS OF UTOPIA

Hope, alongside faith and love, is at the heart of Christianity. Without the hope that good can be sustained, that injustices will be righted, there could not be the spirit to work for justice and peace in the world. Visions of a utopian world in which all is right both evoke and sustain hope. Questions of value are bound to be raised when discussing visions of the future, for instance, What is wrong with today's world? What is right about it? What do we want for our future?

Isaiah's Dream

Purpose

to explore one vision of an ideal world

Preparation

Prepare swords and spears (real or toy ones), pictures of sickles and a plough.
Find the two passages from Isaiah

Assembly

Leader:

There are two sorts of dreams aren't there? There are the dreams which visit us at night when we are fast asleep. Often they are all mixed up and topsy turvey. Sometimes they can be frightening and we call them nightmares.

But there is another sort of dream. It's when we think of how we would like the world to be in the future.

Many, many hundreds of years ago the prophet Isaiah had a dream of the future because when he looked about him there were many things which made him very sad and which he would have liked to change. Although things were very different from today: there were no cars, no computers, no running water in taps, some things were the same – children quarrelled with each other, adults argued, and there were wars. The weapons were different, spears instead of bombs, swords instead of guns, but men and women and children still died because of them. Even animals seemed to be at war with one another as they seem to be today, wolves hunted lambs and tore them to shreds, snakes were deadly poisonous.

But Isaiah had a dream of the future. He said that one day there would come a time when all the living world would be at peace.

Imagine it as Isaiah dreamed it. Instead of the wolf eating the lamb they would live together. The black panther that stealthily preys on baby goats, would lie down next to them and sleep. The calf and the lion cub would feed together. The cow and the bear would be friends. Children would play with the wild animals and not be harmed.

Read Isaiah 11:6–9

And as for the spears and the swords the weapons of war, the people would take the spears and change them into sickles, great curved knives to cut the corn. They would take the swords and hammer them into ploughs to dig up the soil. The weapons which once killed would make tools to grow food for living. No-one would fight with each other any more and no-one would learn how to fight ever again. Discord would be banished forever.

Read Isaiah 2:2–4

Isaiah's dream hasn't come true yet, has it? Children still quarrel. Adults still argue and the news on television reminds us of the many wars which still go on.

But there are people working towards making Isaiah's dream come true. People who work to help men, women and children from different countries become friends. Teachers who try and help children play together co-operatively.

Others who try and teach us to live at peace with animals instead of hurting them.

And we can join in trying to work for Isaiah's dream. Maybe some of you are doing that already?

Prayer/reflection

Lets think of all those who suffer because Isaiah's dream hasn't come true yet. Children who are bullied in playgrounds; children who are hurt when grown-ups quarrel; children who are wounded in wars.

Let's try and be children and adults who try to work for peace and let's start here in school.

Songs

Alleluya

45 Last night I had the strangest dream

Come and Praise

142 I'm gonna lay down my sword and shield
146 We ask that we live and we labour in peace
149 And everyone beneath the vine and the fig tree
83 I'm going to paint a perfect picture

Follow-up

Give children a photocopied page with a picture of the globe in the middle. Ask them to write around it what sort of world they would like to live in.

Discuss with the children whether Isaiah's vision was a realistic one. What was he trying to picture symbolically?

The Amulet

The previous assembly focuses on a general vision. Edith Nesbit's vision in *The Story of the Amulet* (Puffin, 1986) is a specific one. She identified particular things she thought needed to change.

Purpose

to look at specific suggestions for an ideal society

Assembly

Refer to the previous assembly, if you have used it, and explain that Isaiah lived a long time ago, but since his time other people have shared his dream. Some people have also dreamed for themselves about changes they would like to see in the world.

Leader:

Nearly a hundred years ago a woman called Edith Nesbit wrote a book called *The Story of the Amulet* about five children who could travel in time. Usually they travelled to the past but once they travelled to the future. When she wrote about this journey Edith Nesbit was writing of her dream of the future. This is a part of it:

The children found they were in a beautiful park where everything was fresh and green. Around them there were children playing and singing and laughing. Nobody seemed anxious or cross or annoyed, everybody was calm and peaceful. Suddenly there was an unexpected hush and with it the sound of quiet sobbing. Behind a bush a boy was crying.

'Why, whatever is the matter?' asked Anthea, the elder of the two girls.

'I've been expelled from school,' the boy replied.

The children looked at each other. Expelled from school! This was terrible. He must have done something awful to be expelled from school.

'Why, what did you do?' they asked, waiting to hear of some dreadful deed.

'I tore up a piece of paper and dropped it in the playground.'

This was astonishing. Fancy being expelled from school for that! Robert and Cyril both thought guiltily of the sweet wrappers they had dropped that very morning.

'It's only for the day,' said the boy, 'and it is nearly over.'

The children sighed with relief and Robert said, 'Why, lucky you, it's just like a holiday.'

'Oh no,' said the boy. 'It's not a holiday. A holiday is when all your friends are off school too and there are games and parties. Besides, school is so interesting and you can choose what you want to study as well as reading and writing. I'm building a model of a railway and now I will get behind with my project.'

The children thought of their own boring school, where they sat in rows writing all day. They were envious . . .

This was Edith Nesbit's dream of the future. A world in which no-one dropped any litter and where everything would be clean and beautiful. Children would love school and enjoy learning. Perhaps that has come true for many children. She also wrote about homes. She said that all the furniture would be soft and curved so that no children would ever bump their heads. Has that come true? She said that there would be no more coal fires in houses but pipes would carry hot water around the house to heat it instead. Has that come true in your house? Remember, she wrote a hundred years ago. She hoped there would be no more accidents with fire. In her story everybody in the future had comfortable homes. Sadly, that bit hasn't come true. There are many people who have no homes at all today.

Think about what you would like to be different when you grow up. What would you like to change for the better?

Prayer/reflection

Read again Isaiah's vision of a just future. (Isaiah 2:2–4; 11:6–9)

Songs

Come and Praise

42 Travel on, travel on, there's a river that is flowing

47 One more step along the world I go

Follow-up

Ask children to identify one thing in their home or community which would improve the quality of life for some people who live there. They could then draw how it could be improved.

Alternatively ask them to be time travellers reporting back about how things have improved in the future.

FEARS

Fears are often irrational though they can be deep-seated and affect a person's ability to manage their life. These two assemblies are about living with fears. However, do let the stories speak for themselves rather than drawing out a moral from them, otherwise there is a risk of intimidating, rather than helping, the child.

Gandhi

Purpose
to look at one way of coping with fear

Preparation
Prepare to talk about a fear or phobia of yours, preferably one you still have, or alternatively one you suffered from as a child.

Obtain a picture of Gandhi (or Ben Kingsley in the role).

Assembly
Leader:

What are you frightened of? People can be afraid of many different things – of the dark, of spiders, of snakes, of bullies. I myself am frightened of ——. You are probably brave about some things and afraid of other things. And of course there are some things that it is sensible to be frightened of. If you were in danger, it might make good sense to run away.

People who seem very brave or who do brave things are often very frightened underneath. People learn different ways to control their fear. Some people try to pretend they are not frightened, and often find that when they pretend, they feel less afraid! Other people find it helps to talk to someone else about their fears, and they then find it easier to face their fears. Many people pray about their fears.

Here is a story about someone who did brave things but was frightened underneath:

Gandhi was a great Hindu leader and teacher who lived in India earlier this century. He taught people to struggle for what is right, not by fighting, but by bravely resisting what is wrong. Millions of people listened to his teaching, and they called him Mahatma – great soul.

He said that you must not ignore or run away from people doing bad things. He taught that it takes a brave person to fight against thieves and bullies, but it takes an even braver person to stand in their way without fighting. You may get hurt, but if you do not hit back, the people attacking you will see your inner strength. They might even learn from it.

People watched Gandhi and his followers as they faced angry people with sticks and stones, or soldiers with guns. They had no weapons, and they made no move to escape or defend themselves. Everyone was amazed at Gandhi's bravery.

But he was not always so brave. As a child, Gandhi was very shy, and would run home from school very quickly rather than stop to talk with the other children. He was also afraid of the dark, and was terrified that ghosts were hiding in dark corners. But Rambha, an old servant of his family, taught him what to do.

'Whenever you are frightened, pray to Lord Rama,' she said. 'Repeat his name, and remember that he is always with you. He will protect you.'

So whenever he was afraid, Gandhi would pray the name of the god Rama. It helped him go on to face his fears and help many people.

Songs
Come and Praise

48 Father hear the prayer we offer
44 He who would valiant be
56 The Lord's my shepherd
68 Kum ba yah (Adapt the words to include Someone's frightened, Lord)

Alleluya
51 It's me O Lord

Also sing *We shall overcome* by Pete Seeger

Prayer/reflection

Listen to these words of Gandhi's:

> 'Non-violence is a power which can be wielded equally by all – children, young men and women or grown up people – provided they have a living faith in the God of Love and have therefore equal love for mankind. When non-violence is accepted as the law of life it must pervade the whole being and not be applied to isolated acts.'
>
> 'Passive resistance is an all-sided sword; it can be used anyhow; it blesses him who uses it and him against whom it is used. Without drawing a drop of blood it produces far-reaching results. It never rusts and cannot be stolen.'
>
> 'My non-violence does not admit running away from danger and leaving dear ones unprotected.'

Taken from *All Men are Brothers*, excerpts from Gandhi's writings, ed. Krishna Kripalani (Unesco, 1969)

Follow-up

Introduce the Psalms by explaining that they are hymns written thousands of years ago. Many of them are prayers written by someone who was frightened, but knew that God would help him.

Then select from the following for your reading.

Psalm 3:1–6
Psalm 17:9–14
Psalm 22:1–24
Psalm 27
Psalm 31:1–5
Psalm 61:1–5
Psalm 71:1–6
Psalm 91
Psalm 121

Find out more about Gandhi for a class biographical display.

Yu Yu and the Tiger

Purpose
to explore how fear can sometimes be used to advantage

Assembly
Leader:

In the story of Gandhi we saw one way that people can get over their fears: by praying. But sometimes your fear can actually help you get out of a tricky situation – some people even find that being frightened makes them more quick-witted. This traditional story from China is one example:

Yu Yu, the spotted deer, lived near a deep, dark forest. One day a dog chased Yu Yu and he ran away terrified into the forest. He ran blindly into the overhanging creepers, charged head first into thick tree trunks and fell tumbling down into mossy ditches. When his eyes eventually adjusted to the darkness in the forest, he tried to find his way back to his sunny home but he only stumbled deeper and deeper into the forest.

Several hours later Yu Yu entered a clearing and as he raised his head he gazed directly into the hard, glistening, green eyes of a tiger. Yu Yu was terrified and knew that the tiger could kill him with one blow of its powerful paws. But the tiger didn't move a muscle. He had never before seen anything like this creature.

'Why are you so ugly?' demanded the tiger.

Yu Yu was quivering with fear but he didn't want to show it and replied confidently,

'I am Yu Yu, a spotted deer.'

'Oh, so you're a spotted deer,' growled the tiger. 'Well tell me, what are those plants growing out of the top of your head?'

While Yu Yu was desperately trying to think how to explain about his antlers, the tiger crept towards him. Then, just as Yu Yu was about to collapse with terror, he hit upon a clever idea.

'You mean to tell me that you don't know what these simple things are? They are tiger chop sticks. Because tiger meat is so smooth I have to eat it with curved chop sticks which prevent the meat slipping back into my bowl.'

The tiger was startled, but he saw the deer's slight build and gentle eyes and began to doubt Yu Yu's words.

'You're too small to kill a tiger,' he said.

'What do you mean, I'm too small to kill a tiger,' said Yu Yu. 'Just look at these spots on my back. They represent the number of tigers that I've killed and eaten.'

As Yu Yu spoke he began to shake violently and once again the tiger grew suspicious.

'If you are able to kill and eat tigers, why are you trembling?' the tiger asked.

'I'm not trembling,' replied Yu Yu with an unsteady voice.' Before I eat a tiger I have to build up my energy. I'm quivering with force not with fear.'

The tiger didn't wait to hear any more; he just turned on his heels and fled into the forest without a backward glance. The tiger ran and ran until he was sure that the deer had lost track of him and then fell breathlessly under the branches of a pine tree.

'Hello, King Tiger,' cried a voice from above his head. 'You're obviously trying to escape someone. Who are you afraid of?'

The tiger looked upwards and saw a monkey. Stammering and stuttering, he told his strange story.

'I don't believe you,' said the monkey when he had finished. 'Take me to see this strange creature!'

'No, I refuse to go,' snapped the tiger. 'What if the deer attacks me, I've no escape? At least you can climb to safety up a tree.'

But the monkey wouldn't take no for an answer and he begged and begged until the tiger finally agreed to take him.

'But only on one condition,' said the tiger. 'You must strap yourself to my back so that when you swing yourself up into the branches, you'll take me with you.'

The monkey agreed, and as soon as he was securely tied to the tiger's back with thick creepers, they made their way back to the clearing.

Yu Yu lifted his head as he heard a rustle not far away in the shadowy undergrowth, and then he caught a glimpse of the tiger's stripes lit by a shaft of sunlight. Yu Yu screamed with fear and jumped in the air. The tiger, too, leapt in the air with fright. He thought that the deer was summoning up every ounce of energy to kill him and once again the tiger turned on his heels and ran for his life. He charged blindly through bushes, thorns and ditches and all the time the helpless monkey was strapped to his back. Eventually the monkey fainted across the tiger's back and before long the tiger collapsed on the forest floor. When the tiger finally recovered his breath he turned to the monkey.

'I warned you,' he snapped. 'I told you how ferocious the spotted deer is but you wouldn't believe me. Well, from now on you know never to cross its path.'

Adapted from *Chinese Myths and Legends* by Joanne O'Brian (Arrow Books).

Prayer/reflection

Let us think about the story in silence.

Help us, Lord, to face our fears.
Help us to find ways to cope when we are frightened.
Thank you for friends and family to share our fears and help us through them.
Forgive us for the times when our fear makes us do wrong:
when we tell lies,
or desert our friends,
or hurt other people
because we are frightened.

Songs

Come and Praise
48 Father hear the prayer we offer
44 He who would valiant be
56 The Lord's my shepherd
68 Kum ba yah (Adapt the words to include Someone's frightened, Lord)

Alleluya
51 It's me O Lord

Also sing *We shall overcome* by Pete Seeger.

Follow-up

Make puppets to perform the story as a play.

OWNING

These assemblies pick up on a theme on ownership found in the *REAL Infant Assembly Book*. Biblically, the position is that the earth belongs to God and that humanity has stewardship over it. Muslims hold a similar position with the metaphor of vice-regency being the predominant one. These two assemblies raise some issues regarding right ownership.

The Golden Earth

This story also reflects on attitudes to the land, and so could be used in the 'Natural World' section of this book.

This story presents a positive image of Ethiopian culture and heritage which counteracts the often negative one encountered in the media, because of famines in the country.

Purpose
to reflect on the ownership of land

Assembly
Leader:

What is important to you? What would upset you if it were stolen or taken by mistake? Listen to this story and find out from it what was important to the Ethiopians.

The people say that once two European explorers came to Ethiopia. They were seen going north to south, visiting every corner of the vast country. Everywhere they went they made maps of its mountains, roads and rivers.

Word came to the Negus, or Emperor. After hearing about the two men who were making maps, the Emperor sent a guide to help them. When, after several years, the Europeans were through with their task, the guide went back to Addis Ababa and reported to the Emperor what he had seen.

'Everything they have seen, they have written down,' the guide said. 'They have looked at the beginnings of the Nile at Lake Tana and followed the river down from the mountains. They have surveyed the rocks for gold and silver. They have charted the roads and trails.'

The Emperor reflected on the work the Europeans were doing. At last he sent for them so that he might see them before their departure from the country. When they came he greeted them, fed them, and gave them valuable gifts. And when they went to the seashore to board their ship, he sent an escort with them.

As the explorers were about to leave, the Emperor's servants stopped then and removed their shoes. They scrubbed the shoes carefully and returned them to the Europeans.

The Europeans were perplexed, thinking it was a strange Ethiopian custom.

'Why do you do this?' they asked.

And the Emperor's messengers replied: 'Our Emperor has told us to wish you a safe voyage homeward, and to say this to you:

You come from a far-off and powerful country. You have seen with your own eyes that Ethiopia is the most beautiful of all lands. Its earth is dear to us. In it we plant our seed and bury our dead. We lie on it to rest when we are weary, and and graze our cattle on its fields. The trails you have seen from the valleys to the mountains, and from the plains to the forests, they have been made by the feet of our ancestors, our own feet, and the feet of our children. The earth of Ethiopia is our father, our mother, and our brother. We have given you hospitality and valuable gifts. But the earth of Ethiopia is the most precious thing we own, and therefore we cannot spare even a single grain of it.'

From *The Fire on the Mountain* by H. Courlander (Holt, Rhinehart and Winston, 1950)

Prayer/reflection

Every part of this earth is sacred.
Whatever befalls the earth befalls the children of the earth.
The air is precious;
for all of us share the same breath.
This we know, the earth does not belong to us:
we belong to the earth.
This we know, all things are connected;
like the blood which unites one family.
Our God is the same God,
whose compassion is equal for all.
For we did not weave the web of life:
we are merely a strand in it.
Whatever we do to the web,
we do to ourselves.

From *Bread of Tomorrow* ed. Janet Morley (SPCK/Christian Aid, 1992)

Song

Come and Praise
11 For the beauty of the earth
(and others from the Created World section)

Follow-up

Give the children an opportunity to draw a picture of a place which is important to them and talk about why.

The Rabbi and the Pearl

This story questions whether finders are keepers and this question could be posed at the start of the assembly. It also looks at the idea that morality and learning go hand in hand, paralleling the story 'The Wise Teacher' in the *REAL Infant Assembly Book*.

Purpose
to reflect on the saying 'finders keepers'

Assembly
Leader:

Do you know the saying, 'finders keepers, losers weepers'? What do you think it means? How do you feel when you have lost something? What do you do when you find something? This is a story about that problem.

Long ago there lived a famous Jewish teacher, called Simeon Ben Shaler. He was very poor but he wouldn't accept any payment from his pupils.

'My teachers gave me the gift of learning,' he told them. 'Now I give it as a gift to you.'

To earn money to buy food he did all kinds of humble tasks, for example, chopping wood and carrying water from the well for his neighbours. One day his students persuaded him to accept as a gift a donkey they had bought from a trader in the market place. That evening, whilst tending the animal, Simeon found a small leather purse fastened round his neck; inside was a pearl. The students were delighted.

'Now you can sell the pearl and you will never be poor again,' they said.

'But the pearl belongs to the man who sold you the donkey,' protested Simeon.

'The trader sold us the whole donkey, so the pearl is yours. According to the law you need not return it,' the students explained.

Simeon shook his head.

'Oh, what use is all my learning if I do not act rightly towards another person?'

He took the purse and its contents back to the market place where he found the trader and returned it to him. The trader was astonished at Simeon's honesty.

Prayer/reflection
Listen to one of the sayings of a wise Rabbi called Ben Zoma:

Who is really wise?
The person who learns from everyone.
Who is really mighty?
The person who doesn't give into wrong impulses.
Who is really rich?
The person who rejoices in what they have.
Who is really honoured?
The person who honours others.

Song
Come and Praise
50 When a knight won his spurs

Follow-up
Discuss the following talking points: Of what use is learning? Do you have a right to things that you find? What should you do about them?

WISE AND FOOLISH

The idea that one can learn from the fool has been a recurring theme within Christianity. Seemingly foolish behaviour can highlight the paradoxes within an ethical position or can give another sharp perspective on it. In both examples below, one would hope the children would be left feeling puzzled as to whether the central character was wise or foolish.

Brother Juniper

Purpose

to reflect on the wisdom or foolishness of generosity

Assembly

Leader:

Brother Juniper was one of the most famous companions of St. Francis. He was clearly, to say the least, not very bright, but he loved Francis and he loved God, and in time became known throughout Italy as a saint because of his innocence and humility. There are many stories told about him.

Brother Juniper always had a great concern for the poor and needy, so much so, that whenever he came across a poor person who had not enough clothes to keep warm, Brother Juniper would take off his own friar's habit and give it to them. Eventually his superior told Juniper that he was not to give his habit away to anyone. So from then on, Juniper began to give away half of his habit to wrap a poor person in, or his tunic. Exasperated, the superior told him that he was not to give away any of his clothing whatsoever.

A few days later, Brother Juniper was out, and he met a poor man who had nothing but a few rags to wrap himself in.

'For the love of God,' implored the poor man. 'Give me something to keep myself warm!'

Brother Juniper did not know what to do. His superior had told him not to give anything away, but the man had asked him in the name of God. How could he refuse?

'I'll tell you what,' said Juniper, 'I'm not allowed to give you my tunic or my habit, but if you take the tunic off me, I shan't try to stop you!'

So the beggar eagerly pulled off Juniper's tunic, and once more Juniper returned to the house where he lived with the other friars.

'What happened to your tunic this time?' they asked him.

'A good man took it off my back!' he answered.

So kind-hearted was Juniper that he gave away anything he could get hold of to give to the poor. The other friars despaired of him. All they could do was hide anything that was of value. They knew that Juniper gave things away for the love of God and for God's glory, but . . . couldn't they keep *anything* to feed and clothe themselves?

Read Matthew 19:16–22 (The rich young ruler). Explain to the children it was this passage that inspired Saint Francis and Brother Juniper to give away anything they owned.

Follow-up

Talk about the story together. What would you have done if you were Brother Juniper? What would you have said to him if you were his superior?

Levelling the Mountain

Adapted from a story told by the Chinese Taoist philosopher Lieh Tzu.

Purpose
to reflect on the wisdom or foolishness of ambitious projects

Assembly
There is a saying from the Bible that faith can move mountains. Listen to the faith of one old man.

An old man once lived at the foot of a mountain. The mountain was thousands of feet high and many miles round. It barred his way to the river. It made each journey long and tedious. He often shook his fist at the mountain and grumbled.

One day he had an idea.

'Why don't we level the mountain?' he suggested. 'We could take all the soil and sand and rock and dump it in the sea.'

His wife laughed at him. 'You fool!' she said. 'You have barely the strength to lift a bucket. You would be exhausted shifting an ant's hill. What a joke!'

But the old man was determined. He set to work with his son and grandson. They filled up buckets with stones and earth from the mountain and carried them to the sea. A young boy, a neighbour's son, came to help.

Another old man, a wise old man, came to watch. He, too, laughed at the old man attempting to level the mountain.

'You fool!' he mocked. 'You think you can move a mountain. You will never be able to move even a small fraction of the mountain. You are old and feeble. The mountain is too big.'

'You think you are so wise but you are the fool,' answered the old man as he heaved another bucket on to his shoulder. 'Even my neighbour's son knows more than you do. When I die, my son and grandson will go on working, and after them their sons and their sons' sons and so on for many generations. The mountain will not grow any bigger, so why shouldn't we be able to flatten it in the end?'

The wise man could make no reply.

Song
Come and Praise
61 All over the world (the building song)

Follow-up
Encourage the children to try and think of things that take a long time to change but would change if everyone helped.

MIRRORS

The mirror is the central metaphor for the assemblies which follow. They could be linked as a sequence, picking up on the theme of ways of seeing or not seeing ourselves. Or use separately to allow the stories to speak for themselves.

Narcissus

This Greek myth, among its many facets of meaning, expresses the idea, also found in Christianity, that self-absorption can lead to self-destruction – but for it to have any real meaning to the children, they will need to draw their own conclusions from the story.

Purpose

to think about self-absorption

Assembly

Leader:

Narcissus was a handsome youth. People turned their heads and stared when he walked by. They were dazzled by his beauty. They liked to be near him; if he deigned to smile at them they felt blessed by the gods; if he scorned them they crept away and cried.

And he scorned them often. All the adoration made him vain and conceited. He cared only for himself, and nothing for others, he was the centre of his whole world. One nymph whom he had spurned prayed to the goddesses of love that Narcissus's beauty and love of self would be his downfall, and in the end they were.

One spring day Narcissus came across a pool so clean and clear that gazing into it was like gazing into a shiny mirror. Narcissus bent over to look into it and for the first time he got a good look at his own face. He was enchanted by it. He lay down by the pool to look more closely and became transfixed by his own beauty. He stared and stared and stared into the pool, all his attention absorbed. He did not notice the sun sinking behind the horizon; the light of the moon was enough to see by; he did not notice that he had not eaten or drunk anything; he did not hear the voice of a young woman calling to him; he could not be distracted; the beauty of his own face had ensnared him.

Gradually he simply faded away and died from lack of food and drink; but the gods took pity on him and turned him into the beautiful delicate flower, the narcissus that bends and sways by the water as if trying to catch a glimpse of its own reflection.

Songs

Come and Praise

89 Guess how I feel

91 You can build a wall around you

Nathan and David

This could also be adapted to think about abuse of power.

Purpose
to think about seeing yourself and your behaviour in a new light

Assembly
Introduce the following as a story adapted from the Bible:

King David was king of the Jews about three thousand years ago. When he was still a young man, some say still a boy, he had killed a giant with a stone hurled from a catapult. He captured the hill city of Jerusalem and made it his capital. He also loved to play the harp, and wrote hymns, some of which are in the Bible. He loved God and tried to be wise and just in all that he did. But there was a time when he acted neither wisely nor justly.

His palace was on a hill and from it he could see down into many parts of the city. Once, as he stood surveying the houses below, he caught sight of a beautiful woman. Immediately he wanted her for himself. It did not matter that she was the wife of a soldier, Uriah the Hittite; he was the king and he wanted her and so Bathsheba, for that was her name, was summoned to his presence.

Soon he wanted to marry her. She became pregnant so he wanted to marry her even more. But what was he to do about it? Then he had an idea. He would send Uriah to the front of the battlelines in the next battle. Then he would be sure to be killed.

So that is what he did. He ordered that Uriah should be put right in the front of the battle, where the fighting was likely to be very fierce.

As David had hoped, Uriah died in the battle, and David prepared to marry Bathsheba. Then the prophet Nathan came to him and told him this story:

'In your kingdom there is a rich man,' he said 'who has dozens of sheep, lambs and cattle. Next door to him there once lived a poor man who had one lamb that he looked after himself from the time it was born, and he loved it. One night the rich man wanted some meat, so he sent his servants to the poor man's house. They killed the poor man and stole his lamb for the rich man to eat.'

King David was furious.

'Who is he?' he demanded. 'Bring him to me instantly, for he must be punished!'

Quietly Nathan replied,

'You are the man. You could have married almost any woman in the kingdom, but you wanted Bathsheba. Uriah loved Bathsheba and had no-one else, but you killed Uriah to get Bathsheba for yourself. You have done wrong, and God is very angry with you.'

David immediately realised how bad he had been, and prayed to God:

'Have mercy on me, O God, in your goodness,
in your great tenderness wipe away my faults;
wash me clean from my guilt,
purify me from my sin.
For I am well aware of my faults,
I keep thinking about the wrong I have done,
For I have sinned against none other than you,
I have done what you regard as wrong.
God, create a clean heart in me,
put into me a new and constant spirit.
Do not turn away from me.'

Leader:

He wrote these words down and you can read them in Psalm 51 in the Bible.

Sometimes hearing a story can make us think about ourselves. It is like looking in a mirror, you can see your faults. When you look in a mirror you can see if your face is dirty or your hair is untidy. When you listen to a story about other people you can sometimes see your own faults. David thought of himself as clever and beyond criticism. When he heard Nathan's tale, it was like looking in a mirror and seeing that really, after all, he could be quite nasty. But at least he could see that he had done wrong and was sorry.

Prayer/reflection
Listen again to part of the psalm.

Icons

Icons are central to the liturgical traditions of Orthodox Christianity. They are seen as a vehicle through which one may glimpse the divine. There are artistic conventions governing the icons, e.g. the eyes always look directly out of the picture.

Preparation

Find an icon or print of an icon of Mary and Jesus. Before the assembly, set up the icon with an unlit candle or nightlight in front of it.

Purpose

to think about seeing yourself or your behaviour in a new light

Assembly

While the children are watching, quietly light the candle.

Ask the children about the picture, and then explain to them that it is a picture (or copy of one) called an icon. Icons are loved by Christians in Russia, Greece and the Middle East, and found in many churches and homes.

Some say that an icon is like a misted-over mirror – through it you can see a faint reflection of heaven or a glimpse of God's holiness. And, like a mirror, you only see a part. After all, you can never see the front of someone and the back of them at the same time in one mirror.

An icon is a bit like when someone smiles at you in a mirror. You can't see the real person but you can see what sort of mood they're in by the expression on their face. For many Christians an icon is like this. The person praying can feel God's love and grace coming to them through it, almost as if He is talking to them.

It can also be like looking at a mirror in another way. Sometimes when you look in the mirror you see something about your appearance that you hadn't noticed before. Contemplating an icon can be similar. You may realize things about yourself that you hadn't realized before.

There are lots of miracle stories told about icons. How God healed people through them or protected them from danger. In one story the icon even spoke. This is the story.

Once there was a man who lived by attacking people on the roadside and stealing all they had. Despite his wicked ways this robber loved Mary, the mother of Jesus, very much. He had a beautiful icon of her, sitting with her baby Jesus on her knee. Everyday he lit candles before the icon and prayed that Mary would protect him as he went about his day's work, robbing and plundering. Everyday when he had finished his robbing and his pockets were bulging with gold he returned to his icon and knelt before it, and he thanked Mary for taking care of him.

But one evening as he knelt before the shrine, it seemed to him that Mary spoke to him. She said to him, 'Look, look at what you are doing to my child!'

The robber looked up. There on the outstretched hands of the baby, he saw scars; scars which looked as though they had been made by nails driven into the flesh.

He was very angry.

'Who has dared do this to your son!' he thundered. 'Who has dared harm your child? Tell me and I will take my revenge for you!' And even as he spoke, his hand reached for his sword.

'You have,' Mary replied. 'In your beating and your stealing you have harmed my child.'

Then the robber saw that when he had attacked people on the roadside it was as though he had been attacking Jesus Christ himself.

It was as though he had seen himself in a mirror for the first time. He realized what sort of person he was; and he was sorry for what he had done. He stopped stealing and used his money to build an orphanage.

Prayer/reflection

Listen to two prayers which have been used by Christians for hundreds of years, and are especially popular in Greece and Russia. The robber might have said these prayers when he decided to change his ways.

The first is known as the Jesus prayer.

Lord Jesus Christ, Son of God, have mercy on me, a sinner

Kyrie Eleison, Lord have mercy, *Christe Eleison*, Christ have mercy, *Kyrie Eleison*, Lord have mercy.

(The Greek words or the English are often used in Christian services.)

BEING THANKFUL

Saying grace before a meal is an expression of thankfulness for one thing that life offers. This notion of thankfulness, of seeing life as a blessing, permeates the Jewish faith (there are blessings for most occasions) and is an attitude to life held by many Christians as a result of their faith. These, of course, are only a few examples of things for which one might be thankful.

When Sound Stops

Purpose
to give thanks for sounds and silence

Preparation
1. In class, children could make an orchestrated poem together about noises that drive them mad and which they are glad when they stop. For example: a baby crying (someone imitates the noise of a baby crying); alarm bells ringing (a recording or percussion instruments imitating the sound).
2. Make a class poem about the noises the children like or welcome, for example, mother's key in the lock.
3. Ask the children to think about times when they like to be alone in silence, and to describe it, or find poems or passages from books describing something similar.
4. The children could take a survey of how many of them like to have music or the television on when they are playing or drawing or doing homework.

Assembly
Briefly introduce the idea of being thankful, explain that sometimes we are thankful when something stops.

Ask the children to present their prepared pieces and talk briefly to the children about the fact that some people never have silence because they have a permanent ringing in the ear. This is called tinnitus. Ironically it often afflicts people who suffer from full or partial deafness.

Next suggest that some people find noise comforting because they are so used to it. Comment on how people from big, noisy cities often find silence very disturbing or frightening. Also mention that people coming from very noisy cities like Hong Kong, sometimes find even big British cities too quiet. Report on the children's survey about who likes to have music on.

Finish with the class poem of noises the children like or welcome.

Prayer/reflection
Listen to this poem which may have been written by St. Columba who spread Christianity through Scotland in the 6th century:

> Delightful it is to stand on the peak of rock, in the bosom of the isle, gazing on the face of the sea.
> I hear the heaving waves chanting a tune to God in heaven; I see their glittering surf.
> I see the golden beaches, their sands sparkling; I hear the joyous shrieks of the swooping gulls.
> I hear the waves breaking, crashing on rocks, like thunder in heaven. I see the mighty whales.
> . . .
> Let me study sacred books to calm my soul; I pray for peace, kneeling at heaven's gates.
> Let me do my daily work, gathering seaweed, catching fish, giving food to the poor.
> Let me say my daily prayers, sometimes chanting, sometimes quiet, always thanking God.
> Delightful it is always to live on a peaceful isle, in a quiet cell, serving the King of kings.

Songs
The Sound of Silence (Simon and Garfunkel).

Come and Praise
60 I listen, and I listen

A Hymn of St. Ambrose

Purpose
to give thanks for sleep

Preparation
Have the words of the hymn of St. Ambrose written out in English and Latin on a poster or overhead transparency.

Creator of the earth and sky,
Ruling the firmament on high,
Clothing the day with robes of light,
Blessing with gracious sleep the night,

That rest may comfort weary men,
And brace to useful toil again,
And soothe away the harassed mind,
And sorrows heavy load unbind:

Day sinks; we thank thee for thy gift;
Night comes; and once again we lift,
Our prayer and vows and hymns that we,
Against all ills may shielded be.

Deus, creator omnium
polique rector, vestiens
diem decoro lumine,
noctem soporis gratia,

Artus solutus ut quies
reddat laboris usui
mentesque fessas allevet
luxusque solvat anxios;

Grates peracto iam die
et noctis exortu preces,
voti reos ut adiuves,
hymnum canentes solvimus.

Assembly
Talk to the children about attitudes to bedtime and refer to the familiar pleas and complaints which are made about it, e.g. 'Can't I just stay up and see the end of this programme, or finish this game,' and, 'But my friends go to bed much later.' Comment on how children often do feel left out because it can seem as though the rest of the household is doing something interesting and exciting while they have to go to bed.

Then express the idea that sleep can sometimes come as a great pleasure and a relief at the end of a long day. Then read the following or tell it in your own words.

Ambrose was a very busy man. He was Bishop of Milan and everyday he would see to people in need, listen to their troubles, hear their sorrows, and help wherever he could. But as well as all this he spent much of the day debating and arguing about the Christian faith, about what Christians should believe, for he lived in the fourth century which was a time when Christian leaders were very concerned about such matters. Sometimes when he went to bed he must have been very tired indeed, maybe he had a headache because everyone had been talking to him so much. Then he would feel so grateful that sleep would overwhelm him so that he could gain rest and start each day afresh.

We know he felt that way because he wrote a hymn in which he thanks God for sleep. He wrote it in Latin, but in English he says,

> 'Clothing the day with robes of light
> Blessing with gracious sleep the night.'

Another church father, Bishop Augustine, wrote in his autobiography how he found great comfort in those words on the night of his mother's funeral. He tossed and he turned until he remembered Ambrose's words as though in a dream, and they helped him slip into the warm comfort of sleep.

In the Muslim holy book the Qur'an there is a similar idea expressed, a similar giving thanks for God and that each day starts afresh:

And it is He who makes the night as a robe for you, and sleep as repose and makes the day as it were a resurrection. (Surah 25:47)

Prayer/reflection
Ask the children to shut their eyes and imagine sleep coming down over them like a blanket or coat.

Then read the words of the hymn again.

Follow-up
Discuss with the children their thoughts about sleep, covering such points as: Is sleep always restful? What about dreams and nightmares? How do they feel when they wake up? Do they like going to bed?

Ask them to write a simple poem about sleep.

Ask the children to make a symbolic picture of the night as a robe and sleep as a gift or blessing.

The Clown of God

This links with an assembly on 'Laughter' in the *REAL Infant Assembly Book.*

Purpose

to celebrate skills and gifts which may be unappreciated

Assembly

Leader:

It was time for the festival in the little town. Every year the people gathered to give honour to Mary, the mother of Jesus. Her statue stood in the parish church, it was a tall, serious figure holding the baby Jesus in her arms. People would come from miles around to give gifts in honour of Mary, and the gifts would be used to help the poor, or to make the church more beautiful. Everyone tried to bring a better gift than anyone else, and it was said that if a gift was especially pleasing to Mary, then her face in the statue would seem to smile.

All day people streamed into the town. The rich were the first to parade before the statue. They laid beautiful robes, jewels, food and money before the statue, and as they did so, each one looked at what others had brought, and thought, 'Mine's the best. The statue will smile for me!' But no matter how lovely or expensive the gifts were, Mary did not smile.

The merchants came next, offering all manner of delicate objects or great rolls of cloth, vying with each other to bring the most unusual and interesting things they had found in their travels. But still Mary did not smile.

Throughout the day, people brought their gifts and laid them before Mary, but she did not smile. That night, the people went home wondering what could make Mary smile if it was not any of the riches and delights which they had brought.

One man had not laid anything before the statue. He was an old man whose entire life had been spent as a clown, a juggler and a comedian. Now, an old man, he was so poor he had nothing to eat himself, let alone anything to give to Mary. Ashamed of his poverty, he waited until everyone had gone home. Then he crept into the church. A candle glowed beside the statue, illuminating the sad face of Mary. The clown stood before her and said,

'Holy Mother, I am a poor man. I have no gold or jewels, cloth or riches to lay before you. I would like to be able to help the poor or make your church more beautiful, but I have nothing to give you. All I have ever been able to do is sing, and dance, and tell jokes and juggle. It made people laugh, but it never brought me enough to be able to help others. And now I am old I am not much good at entertaining any more. Sometimes people laugh at me because I drop my clubs when I am juggling and forget the words of my songs. But I cannot leave without honouring you with my gift. It is a poor gift, but it is all I have. Maybe you will accept this as a gift for your Holy Child.'

So saying, he bowed and then leapt into the air and turned a somersault. His old bones creaked, but he ignored them. He danced, he juggled, he told jokes, he sang songs. All through the night he performed as he had never performed before. He put body and soul into his old routines until, exhausted by the effort, he collapsed at the feet of the statue.

And it was there that the priest found him the next morning. As he walked in to say his morning prayers, he was shocked to see what looked like an old tramp, lying on the floor. He was just about to wake him up and tell him to get out, when he looked up at the statue. To his amazement and delight, he saw that Mary was smiling. The old clown woke up and looked up at the statue. Turning in astonishment to the priest he said, 'She is smiling! What wonderful gift has she been given?'

Prayer/reflection

Let us value ourselves and our skills, and use them to help others. Let us value the gifts and skills of others, and encourage others in whatever they can offer.

Songs

Come and Praise
22 Lord of the dance
59 The best gift

Follow-up

Help the children prepare a variety show which they can then present to the rest of the school in an assembly. Encourage participation from everyone, using a variety of skills.

PEOPLE WHO ARE REMEMBERED

Every age and culture has its heroes and heroines, or people who are remembered for one reason or another. These two assemblies present contrasting models of a person worth remembering. Other assemblies in this book, for example, 'Gandhi' or 'One Thousand Deaths', can also fit in with this theme, as well as stories of your own favourite heroes and heroines.

To introduce any of the following assemblies, first talk to the children briefly about heroes and heroines; what sort of characteristics should they have? Ask the children why we should praise or respect people. You could mention popular reasons why people are lauded, perhaps questioning some of these e.g. because they are rich or because we see them on the television.

Horatio Defends the Bridge

Purpose
to look at one example of fighting for a cause

Assembly
Make a general introduction to the theme of heroes and heroines then tell the following story.

Many people like to tell stories of men and women whose bravery has been praised for many generations. The ancient Romans told a story about Horatio who was a soldier in the Roman army. One day he was guarding the wooden bridge which spanned the river Tiber. Now this bridge was the only bridge across the Tiber, the great river which cut the city of Rome off from the lands to the north. If you wanted to enter Rome from the north you had to cross over this bridge, there was no other way.

As Horatio stood on duty, gazing into the distance, he suddenly became aware that something was happening in the town on the far bank of the river. He could hear sounds of screaming and fighting. What was going on? Then soldiers from his own army came running in fear and disarray.

Horatio soon learnt that the deadly enemy of the Romans, the Etruscans, had made a surprise attack capturing the town over the river. Now they were advancing on Rome and soon they would reach the bridge.

There was turmoil all around Horatio as Roman soldiers sought to grab their belongings and flee from the enemy. They had been caught unprepared for battle. There was chaos all around. Horatio alone remained calm. He knew instantly what must be done.

'Stop,' he yelled at the top of his voice. 'Stop and destroy this bridge. Burn it, hack it down. Do whatever you can. The bridge must be destroyed or tomorrow the Etruscan army will be walking the streets of Rome. You get to work and I will stop the Etruscans coming over.'

Seizing his sword and shield, Horatio sprang to the far end of the bridge. Two of his friends stood with him. Together they stood side by side barring the way, determined to stop the enemy, determined to save their city. Behind them the Roman soldiers began destroying the bridge.

The forerunners of the Etruscan army attempted to topple the guards from the bridge but Horatio and his friends fought the soldiers off . . . and the next ones and the next ones, and the next ones after them.

The wooden structure of the bridge began to quiver and tremble – the Etruscan troops were drawing near. 'Go to safety,' Horatio urged his companions. They escaped but Horatio remained – he would not move while the bridge still stood.

Seeing him standing there, the approaching

Etruscan army stopped in sheer amazement at such bravery, and such foolishness. But still the advance guard came forward to try to dislodge him, so that their army could pass over. And one by one Horatio knocked them back, mocking them as he did so.

'You're nothing but slaves of a tyrant,' he taunted. 'Slaves who care so little for freedom, you want to take the freedom of others.'

But then the whole Etruscan army began to move forward, hoping to move him out of the way with the weight of their number. They moved forward – one army against a single man.

And behind Horatio the bridge was beginning to collapse.

'Come back, come back Horatio,' cried his friends. But Horatio would not leave his post. The Etruscan army was coming nearer. Horatio stood his ground. They came nearer still and still Horatio stood, a little nearer and they were almost upon him.

There was a loud crack. The bridge plunged into the swirling waters of the river below. Horatio leapt into the waters after it and swam to safety. The Romans cheered and cheered. The city had been saved by the bravery of one man.

Since that time the story of Horatio has been told again and again. It was undoubtedly told by the Romans who came to Britain. Strange, isn't it, though, to think they were so proud of a man who defended freedom. After all they cared little for the freedom of the Britons they had conquered.

Prayer/reflection

Ask the children to sit and think about one final point. Does caring about freedom mean you care for the freedom of all peoples and not just the freedom of your own kind?

Then say:

Let us be thankful for all those who have stood up for freedom. Amen

Song

Come and Praise

71 If I had a hammer

Follow-up

Ask children to research the lives of other Roman heroes and heroines and to write stories of their own heroes and heroines.

Read extracts from Macaulay's *Lays of Ancient Rome* where the story is told in verse.

Who Should We Honour?

This also ties in with the topic on 'Money' in the *REAL Junior Teacher's Handbook*.

Purpose

to encourage the children to question the value of wealth and riches and to look at how self-denial is also honoured

Assembly

Use the general introduction about heroes and heroines at the beginning of this section.

Then introduce the idea that some people are remembered for many hundreds of years, not because they are rich or wealthy, but the exact opposite; they are remembered because they thought the most important thing in life was to pray to God and serve the poor. These were people like St. Francis of Assisi or Saint Lucia (see *A Tapestry of Tales*), or Simon Stylites (see *REAL Infant Assembly Book*).

One such holy person was a Muslim woman who lived in the eighth century in Iraq. Her name was Rabi'a. Her parents were poor. They died in a famine. Rabi'a was captured by some bandits and sold as a slave. Her master freed her and it is said that she travelled across the land and beyond, playing on her flute and singing of the love of God. At last, she settled down but her house was only an old tumbledown shack, little more than a ruin.

She was known for her love of God, and one day a wealthy man came to visit Rabi'a. He thought to himself, 'She deserves better than this,' and he gave her enough money to buy a new house.

Rabi'a sat in the house that the rich man wanted her to buy. She gazed in delight at the beautiful paintings on the walls. She stared at its fine fittings and rejoiced at its cool airiness.

Then she left the new house, gave the money back to the rich man, and went to live once more in her old, ruined shack.

'Why wouldn't you live there?' he asked.

'Why wouldn't you live there?' said her friends.

Why indeed?

'Because I was afraid I would fall in love with the house,' replied Rabi'a.

It appears that Rabi'a had many other offers of wealth and marriage but she preferred to live where she could concentrate her love on God rather than on riches.

A rich young ruler once came to Jesus and asked how he could see the kingdom of God. Jesus told him to give away all that he had. The young man went sorrowfully away (Matthew 19:21–22).

Adapted from *Doorkeeper of the Heart*, version of Rabi'a by Charles Upton (Threshold Books, Vermont, 1988)

Prayer/reflection

Listen to what Jesus said to a rich person:
Read Matthew 19:16–22

We give thanks for the good things we have.
Let us honour those who are prepared to give up money and possessions for something better.

Song

Come and Praise
97 'Tis the gift to be simple

MISCELLANEOUS

Comforting

This could be adapted to be an assembly about commemorating important events.

Purpose
to explore some uncomfortable aspects of caring

Preparation
Pictures of the Bayeux tapestry are not strictly necessary but would be very useful.

Assembly
Leader:

There have been Kings and Queens in England for hundreds of years. Today there are strict rules about who will become King or Queen when the old one dies, but this has not always been the case. There were often quarrels about who should be the ruler and often the quarrels turned into wars. This happened nearly a thousand years ago when King Edward the First died.

Two men claimed the throne of England. Two men said it was theirs by right. One was Harold, noble brothdq-in-law and adviser to the king.

He said, 'King Edward named me to be his successor as he lay dying. He said I should inherit the throne. I should be King of all England.'

But across the sea in Normandy, now a part of France, another man was saying 'No, the throne of England is mine. Edward promised it to me, and Harold, too, once swore in a holy oath that he would make no claim on it.'

When Harold's messengers told them what William said, he said, 'Yes, I promised, but William forced me to do so. I didn't make the promise by my own free will, so it doesn't count. England is mine.'

The powerful barons wanted Harold to be their King and Harold was crowned King of England.

But William was not going to give up. He rounded up his army and set sail for England. William's army met Harold's army near Hastings. Harold was killed, (some say an arrow struck him in the eye) and William's army were the victors. William was crowned King and to this day he is known as William the Conqueror.

In his homeland in Normandy everyone was very proud of William, especially his family. They wanted to make something to commemorate William's victory so that people would know he was a hero for a long time to come. They wanted to make the story of his great conquest known. But instead of writing the story or drawing it, they embroidered the story onto cloth. The finished piece was about 75 metres long. You can still see it today in France. You start at the beginning and see King Edward talking to Harold, and at the end you see Harold's soldiers fleeing from the battlefield, and there are many pictures in between. The story is written underneath very simply in Latin.

One picture is very interesting. Underneath it seems to say that Odo, a bishop who supported William, is 'comforting' the soldiers. The Latin word is 'confortat'. Now what would you expect to see in that picture? Perhaps Odo bandaging the wound of one of his soldiers and saying, 'There, there,' but no, it's not that. Perhaps Odo putting his arm round someone as your mum or dad might comfort you, but no, it's not that. Perhaps Odo saying, 'Don't worry everyone, don't be frightened, everything will be all right,' but no, it's not that either.

What the picture shows is Odo brandishing a huge club, rather like an American baseball bat, making sure that his soldiers keep on charging into battle – and some of them don't look too happy about it!

Our word 'comfort' comes from that Latin word, but most people don't use it in that way any more. It meant 'strengthen', or 'encourage'. You have to *con*-fort someone to help them make an *ef*-fort.

There are many ways of strengthening someone. Mothers and fathers and teachers often comfort children by putting their arms around them, or telling them everything will be fine or giving them a hanky to wipe away their tears. Sometimes, though, they have to be like Odo with his troops and comfort children in an old-fashioned sense. No, they don't get behind them with a baseball bat but they have to be strict and insist and say,

'You are just going to get your story written, even if you don't feel like doing it,' or 'You are going to stay on the bike until you learn to ride,' and other things like that, because they know the child will win and learn that way.

Prayer/reflection

Listen to the words of this hymn, and think whether you can agree with it. Then read one or more verses of *Come and Praise* 48: Father hear the prayer we offer.

Songs

Come and Praise

Any hymn from the Journey of Life section, especially:

48 Father hear the prayer we offer

and

50 When a knight won his spurs

Follow-up

Ask children to devise plays showing a parent comforting a child in different ways or follow up the Bayeux tapestry theme and ask children to do individual cartoon strips depicting scenes from their own lives.

Individually or in pairs research the life of someone the children think worthy of commemorating and design a tapestry of something in their lives. As a school effort design a tapestry showing the history of the school.

Follow up the story of the disputed throne.

Discuss making promises with the children. Think of circumstances when it might be right to break a promise.

In Pursuit of True Happiness

The following is a story we have freely adapted from one we heard told by Leslie Wilson. She in turn had freely adapted it from one once heard on the radio.

The theme is one which was implicit in the ministry of Jesus: the kingdom of God, 'true happiness,' is at hand if only you open your eyes to see it. The story of Baboushka in *A Tapestry of Tales* has a related theme.

The ending of this story will no doubt catch children by surprise. They will need to go away and puzzle out a meaning for themselves. It is a story which lends itself to being acted out by children, with a child or teacher as narrator. The repetition of the language should also encourage audience participation.

Purpose

to encourage reflection on true happiness

Assembly

Leader:

A man once sought true happiness. He could not find it in the village where he lived so he set out to seek the advice of the old woman of the far mountains. Her knowledge and wisdom were known throughout the land, and the land beyond and the land beyond that land.

Well, he walked a day and he walked a month and he walked a year and on the way he met a lion.

'Where are you going?' asked the lion.

'I am going to try to find true happiness,' replied the man. 'I am going to seek the advice of the old woman of the far mountains. Her knowledge and wisdom is known throughout this land and the land beyond, and the land beyond that land.'

'Ah, if only I had enough to eat,' sighed the lion, 'then I think I would be happy. Ask her how I can find something to eat which will really make me feel full and satisfied, will you please?'

The man promised and he began his journey once more. He walked a day and he walked a month and he walked a year and on the way he stopped in a village.

This village had been struck by a terrible storm. Crops were ruined. Houses were without roofs and the people were in despair.

When they heard of the man's quest, they too sighed and said, 'Oh, if only we could find the money to repair our roofs and buy food to feed ourselves and our children, then I am sure we could find true happiness! Will you ask the old woman's advice please?'

The man promised and began his journey once more. He walked a day and he walked a month and he walked a year and on the way he met a young woman sitting by the roadside, weeping.

'Why do you weep?' he asked, moved for a moment by pity.

'I am so lonely!' she cried. 'My parents have both died and I have no family.'

'I am going to seek the advice of the old woman of the far mountains,' said the man. 'Her knowledge and wisdom are known throughout this land, and the land beyond, and the land beyond that one. I will ask her for you. Perhaps she can help.'

'Thank you, thank you!' replied the girl.

Now it was the last stage of the journey. He walked a day and he walked a month and he walked a year and now he stood before the old woman of the mountains.

'You seek true happiness,' she said, for of course, her knowledge and wisdom were known throughout the land and the land beyond and the land beyond that one.

'Listen to me carefully. You will find true happiness on your journey home. But you will have to keep your eyes and ears open or you may miss it forever.'

The man thanked her and was about to go when she beckoned him back.

'Weren't there other questions you wished to ask me?' she said. 'Deep desires from other people?'

'Oh yes,' he blushed because he had so nearly forgotten. 'Yes there were.'

So he asked his questions, and the wise woman of the far mountains gave him her replies.

He hurried down the mountain, and on his journey the first person he met was the woman who had been weeping by the roadside.

'Oh!' she called, hurrying to meet him, 'I am glad to see you. I've been waiting for more than a year. Did you ask my question? Did she give you her advice?'

'I did,' announced the man proudly bearing his message. 'She said that you should find a friend, man or woman, to come and live with you and be your companion. Someone kind and gentle. Someone who will walk with you and enjoy the beauty of the woods. Someone to talk with as the sun is setting.'

The woman's face lit up briefly but then it fell again. 'Wise words,' she said, 'But where can I find such a person? I know of no-one round here.' Then she looked at the man. 'Why, I know!' she exclaimed, 'You could come and be my companion. You seem kind and gentle. You like walking in the woods. You stay here and be my companion!'

The man paused for a moment. The thought was tempting. He too had been lonely and it would be good to have someone with whom to share his life. But no, he must continue his quest for true happiness. He bade farewell and set out once again.

When he arrived at the village, he found that things had gone from bad to worse, and the villagers were surprised to see him.

'It's you,' they said, 'It must be four years since you've passed this way. Four years when we have had little food and shelter. Do you have any news for us?'

'I do,' replied the man, 'The wise woman of the far mountains told me that there is a well in your village, a disused well. In its depths there is a treasure of gold, stolen a hundred years ago. The thief and owner are long since dead. It will be enough to mend your homes, buy food, and set up your farms again.'

The villagers were overjoyed but then their gloom returned. 'But we are too weak to haul such treasure from the well.' They looked at the man. 'Why don't you stay with us? You are fit and healthy. You stay with us and help us. It will take some time, we know, but we will share our joy and our wealth with you.'

The man paused, it was tempting, but then he said, 'No, no. I will not stay. You must find someone else to help you. If I do not keep to my journey I might not find true happiness. No, I will keep to my quest.' And he continued his journey.

And again he met the lion. The lion was even thinner and even more hungry than he had been before.

'You took your time,' said the lion. 'Six years I've waited for you. What did the wise woman of the far mountains say?'

'She said I could find true happiness on the way home, but to be careful because I might miss it for ever,' replied the man. 'But I haven't seen it yet.' He stopped thoughtfully a moment, 'At least I don't think I have.'

The lion was impatient, 'No, no, I am not asking about your happiness. I am asking about mine. What advice did the wise woman of the far mountains give to me?'

'Oh,' said the man without thinking, 'She said to eat the first foolish man who came along.'

So the lion ate the foolish man.

Prayer/reflection

Listen to these words of Jesus:

> 'The coming of the kingdom of God is not something you can see, and there will be no-one to say, "Look here! Look there!" for, you must know, the kingdom of God is among you.' (Luke 17:20–21)
>
> May we be always ready to see and hear and understand the good things around us.

Songs

Alleluya

41 Streets of London

Come and Praise

91 You can build a wall around you

Follow-up

Invite a general discussion about the story without imposing a meaning on it.

Encourage the children to articulate orally or in writing their own ideas of what true happiness would be.

CROSS-REFERENCE TABLE

This table shows links between the assemblies and the topics in the *REAL Junior Teacher's Handbook*.

Assemblies / *Topics*	Living World	Local Area	Place of Worship	Names	Water	Friends	Food	Learning	Messages	Writings	Rules	Money	Time	Journeys	Change	Light	Christmas	Passover	Ramadan/Eid	Easter	Baisakhi
New School Year						●		●							●						
God's Suffering																				●	
Saint Hubert																					
St. George's Day																					
Baisakhi																					●
Holi						●															
Remembrance Day																					
Children's Newsdesk		●				●		●													
Assisi Pilgrimage	●													●							
Judgement of Wind	●										●										
A Guide		●	●																		
Local Building		●	●																		
Book of Life						●						●									
Three Friends						●								●							
Bread							●														
Plays Without Words									●												
Lion and Hermit	●					●					●										
Goats Who Killed . . .											●										
Gold into Brass											●	●									
What is the Smell . . .?											●	●									
Change of Heart									●						●						
One Thousand Deaths															●						
Isaiah's Dream										●			●		●						
The Amulet								●					●		●						
Gandhi						●									●						
Yu Yu and Tiger																					
Golden Earth																					
Rabbi and Pearl								●			●	●									
Brother Juniper																					
Levelling Mountain															●						
Narcissus															●						
Nathan and David								●		●	●				●						
Icons								●							●						
When Sound Stops																					
St. Ambrose																					
Clown of God																					
Horatio and Bridge																					
Who Should we . . .?												●							●		
Comforting																					
Pursuit of True . . .																					